There's Nothing Going On But Your Thoughts

Reconcile With Guilt, Anger, Fear and The Past

Book 1

By Helen Gordon

Foreword By Les Brown

PUBLISHED BY
Clearly Written
www.clearly-written.com

Visit our website at www.helengordon.com

There's Nothing Going On But Your Thoughts – Reconcile With Guilt, Anger, Fear and The Past - Book 1/Helen Gordon.

First Edition

ISBN: 978-0615470528
ISBN: 0615470521

Cover Design by Carroll Eristhee

Table of Contents

Acknowledgments

Thank you so much:

David Kensler for getting me out of my comfort zone and started on the path of my dreams. **Barbara Kensler** for her unconditional love and encouragement to write; **Jayne Whittaker** for being the best friend through my transition to writing as a career; my **ACIM students** for urging me to compile my class lectures into a book; **Marie Thomas** for archiving years of my class lectures; **Rev. Daytra Hansel, Alayne Davis** and **Elvira Bohle** for encouragement and prayer; **Maria Sauper, Marilyn Krumrey,** and **Patti Honoré** for editorial review; **Debra Karr** for her inspiration and publishing guidance; **Sean Kelly** for the perfect place to compile this book; and **Les Brown** for believing in my books. I thank **God** for them all.

Foreword

By Les Brown

Most of us have encountered change overnight. At a time when we're shifting from a domestic economy to a global economy, when foreclosures have skyrocketed, and many people are feeling powerless and hopeless, there is a voice of inspiration emerging to the forefront.

In *There's Nothing Going On But Your Thoughts*, author Helen Gordon helps you to reconnect with your personal power. Her practical methods will usher you from vision to completion.

Helen urges you to reflect on your life and determine exactly what needs to be reconciled from the inside out. You will embark on a journey that empowers you to come to grips with your past, celebrate your present, and breakthrough to your future.

Undoubtedly, *There's Nothing Going On But Your Thoughts* will propel you to move forward and free you to "get unstuck". Helen Gordon takes you on an inward voyage of self-discovery by unlocking hidden truths that lead to the manifestation of the greatness within.

Get ready to conquer more than you could ever imagine.

Your past is waiting patiently for your success to begin in you. Helen Gordon gives you the tools to face your history and create a greater reality.

Les Brown
Speaker/Speech Coach/Trainer

Introduction

Do floods of disturbing emotion still rise regarding particular relationships? Are there conflicts you just cannot seem to reconcile? Do you fear the resolution process might be incriminating or painful? Perhaps you feel life just no longer seems necessary nor seems to have much purpose. Are these conflicts controlling your life?

The conflict is not your relationship with someone or something; it is with your relationship with yourself, and it is controlling your life. You have the power to reclaim control of your life in a deliberate, slow and simple way without prior experience. Find that power and learn how to use it.

I will gently guide you as far as you are willing to go in the acceptance of your power to control your life and to end your denial, resistance or fear of this power.

Perhaps you give love more than you allow yourself to receive it. What you will discover in this powerful book is why you have denied love, rejected it, or feared it to such an extent that it seems void in your life.

There's Nothing Going On But Your Thoughts addresses and goes beyond the intellectual understanding of how to find answers and solutions to inner conflicts. Additionally, it provides effective tools to find answers and guidance on what to do with those findings.

To easily apply the solutions, proven exercises guide you in releasing conflict, guilt, anger and the past for a new peace filled life. Life and peace can be given back to you beginning now by privately reconciling with yourself.

Some exercises may seem unnecessary. Remember, these are *new* concepts and perceptions you may find unfamiliar or uncommon. You are releasing the old that has not served you in meeting the goals of the inner peace, health, and prosperity that you desire.

In this process, you unlearn old interpretations to see things as they are, not as they seem. You may discover that you have merely inherited your unwanted behavior, guilt, or anger and no longer have to sustain it. Change happens. Release is inevitable. Your calling is revealed.

Some of the lessons you will find comforting. It is okay to use them when needed in daily situations. This is called applying the principles presented in this text. It is the best way to release the beliefs that are disrupting your life.

Some lessons you might resist for they threaten to open a door that you would prefer to remain closed. Let it open so the frightened little mind can escape its prison.

To benefit fully from this book, put aside all current beliefs, opinions, and definitions regardless of credentials, experiences, facts, or past studies. Gently put them aside somewhere while applying the principles recommended in this book.

Curiosity, an urge, and a little willingness have attracted you to this book to accept more love and its rewards. Expect this willingness to change at times while doing the exercises. This is important to remember. It is common to repeat chapters as willingness changes to accept more joy, healing, and peace of mind. Proceed at your own pace and in private if you choose.

There may be some feelings of resistance and disbelief even while reading this introduction. This is certainly okay and normal! Resistance and anger may come and go; however, things, people, and situations show up to support you through this process. Not to worry. Let them help.

Occasionally, there may be temptation to *go back to old ways* simply because old ways are familiar and comfortable. New things can be uncomfortable at first but it is well worth the wonderful healing as you move through the process.

Ignore the urgencies of your inner critic (ego) while progressing through each chapter. The ego did not take only a few chapters (years) of your life to teach you the way you are living it. Although it is possible to learn these new principles quickly with discipline and commitment, most likely decades of learned behavior probably will not be unlearned overnight. It would be overwhelming.

The good news is, learning comes much faster than expected, expanding more each day. One day you will realize that you finally get it, live it, and love it. You become your own best friend and biggest fan.

As this happens, dependencies of all kinds are subtly abandoned; relationships in conflict are diffused; respect is obtained; self-confidence is strengthened; and love replaces hate. Many good things become free to manifest in your life. Mental freedom happens. Emotional freedom is certain.

Keep reading; your life has already begun to change. Nothing is beyond your reach. Nothing is impossible. No experience necessary. Welcome to the rest of your life!

Christian Terminology

Although Christian terminology is found in this book, it is different from its traditional usage:

- **God** has no gender. When God is referenced using a masculine gender, it is for literary purposes.

- **Sin** is merely an error or misinterpretation. It can be corrected.

- **Salvation** is recognition an error has been made.

- **Atonement** is acceptance the error has been corrected.

- The **Holy Spirit** is your: inner Voice, divine Guide, holy Spirit, and spiritual Being. It is that part of you, which is always in communication with God. It is who you truly are, the voice for God.

- **Forgiveness** is not a pardon, but a correction in perception and the freedom to move on.

- The **ego** is that loud inner critic. Wrong-thinking. Offers unfavorable choices.

- **Illusions** refer to human being experiences.

- **Self**, in upper case, refers to your true Being that guides you rightly and is always in connection and agreement with God. It is not physical.

- **self**, in lowercase, refers to the human personality that is governed by the ego. It is physical.

- **Voice** is your inner guide for right choices, your holy Spirit.

Other Terms:

ACIM: A Course In Miracles. Lessons of forgiveness.

Gender Usage

This book utilizes masculine pronouns, traditionally the preferred usage in English literature, as representing no gender in particular. It may be helpful to mentally substitute those masculine pronouns with words like, *child, daughter, sister, her or she.*

1

Your Gift to the World

The Impossible Dream, Isn't

"Champions aren't made in the gym. Champions are made from something they have deep inside of them--a desire, a dream, a vision. They have to have last-minute stamina, they have to be a little faster, they have to have the skill and the will, but the will must be stronger than the skill."
— *Muhammad Ali.*

You have a dream, an urging to express yourself. Hold on to it for the dream is God's idea eager to be expressed through you. It is God's choice that through you the idea should be fulfilled. God gave you the idea with a restlessness to live it and with the tools, passion, and joy to see it through full manifestation. Through this idea, the grace of God is experienced within all who are exposed to it.

Sure, you have a dream. We all have a dream, a strong desire of some kind, something that provides deep satisfaction. If you feel this does not apply to you, let us help you find your dream. If you know what it is, it is time to enhance it.

Now, this is not a dream of fantasy. It is a physical activity of sorts in our human experience, which takes place while fully awake. The idea may be in the form of a song, a painting, a sculpture, a garment, a poem, a literary work, an oratory, a community service, a recipe, a garden, or many forms but it is the idea of God that ultimately comes forth in all Its splendor.

Perhaps right now we have chosen to deny the dream's existence as if it were our own little secret. Thus, we believe we control when, if ever, it will be exposed to the world. Doing so gives a false sense of control. The dream cannot be controlled or contained within us since it does not belong to us. Remaining closed to the dream does not give us control of it nor can we imprison its divineness.

Our human being is an incubator for the dream and desires to come through us effortlessly. An idea of God eventually emerges from its incubator for it has a purpose in this human experience. Fulfillment of that purpose unfolds regardless of our conscious participation.

We have the opportunity to be the main conduit for the dream to unfold. Simply shoving it deep into our subconscious is an act of denial where insecure thoughts grasp the illusion it knows nothing of the dream. This is a form of fear. We fear clarity of the dream for our knowing dissolves the lies we have created or accepted about ourselves which prevent us from pursuing this desire.

Fear, our worst enemy, tries to convince us of the seeming limitations or impossibilities of reaching our dream's goal. Although we fear failure, God cannot fail Itself. Sometimes those insecure thoughts question our worthiness, playing on the self-created shortcomings we allow in our lives.

Questioning our worthiness says we need somehow to make a change. If there were a need to change something to establish our worthiness, that particular dream would not be so urgent to express through us. Questioning our worthiness also says God did not know what He was doing when He chose us for our role in the dream; He must have made a wrong choice. This is absurd and we no longer allow our fears to imply such an insult to ourselves or to God!

If necessary, a challenge of human preparation, such as formal training, to strengthen our faith in ourselves, may be in order. Training can help release thoughts of limitations. Releasing the limitations haunting our little self frees the power of our higher Self. Progressively, our faith in ourselves strengthens. God's faith in our ability to fulfill our calling, i.e., our role in the dream, is stronger than ours, unshakable and certain of our success.

Regardless of the appearance and seeming influence of the dream, we will be guided and inspired righteously. Others' dreams may appear more significant than ours, so we feel there is some queue for us to wait in before pursuing our dream. All dreams are equal in the eyes of God. God's idea is not in waiting; it is continuously unfolding.

Faith is weakened when concerned with how impossible the dream may seem. There is no impossible dream. God did not create a dream or idea He cannot fulfill. God has no need to fantasize.

We are perfect for our role. This dream was deliberately given through us knowing it can be expressed and manifested best with our particular skill.

Steps toward perfecting this skill progress easily. This skill unfolds happily in the form of a *natural gift*. However, a natural gift is merely a complete inner instruction manual on how to live this dream to its fullest. We have ready access to this inner manual at any instant because it is as much a part of us as the flesh on our body. Inquiries of this inner manual can be made at will. It is always present to support us in every way. This is Its purpose.

But this is too much fun? Desires are meant to be enjoyed; otherwise, they are a chore! Chores are far more difficult to start. God knows that making the dream desirable is an advantage for all.

Go forward with the dream with sincere humility. Humility creates that space in the mind for greatness to express through us. As we fully accept this role of grandeur, God has more grand and glorious things awaiting us.

Acceptance of our abilities in this role allows us to put truth in visible action. From this action, there is divine reaction, the natural unfoldment of abundant blessings. We discover a special joy as we develop the dream.

We cannot help but feel good when engaged in fulfilling the dream because we are fulfilling our calling, God's idea. There is no need to focus on who validates our dream's worth. We are magnificently and wonderfully made for what God has purposed; our existence is not a mistake. Our role is valuable.

Our activities inspire many who in some form or time have the opportunity to witness the joy of our work. Within each one's inspiration is a revelation. Perhaps it is the revelation of our own divine dream.

One dream reveals another; inspires another; prepares for another; unites with another; and is shared with another to expand this idea of God. This idea was established well before our first breath. We had nothing to do with its inception. However, it must be made manifest here on earth.

Reaching the goal of the dream is not the end. It is the beginning of a new one, usually apparent well before the goal is reached. Eventually it is revealed how that goal was merely a stepping-stone for the expansion of the dream.

Commitment to the dream allows us to live in a state of grace for we become aware of the Truth about who we are and our reason for being. Grace becomes obvious to us. The purpose of our dream becomes clear. Our commitment becomes stronger. Life becomes joyful.

Commit to the dream but not for the sake of personal recognition or monetary gain. Commit for the glorification of God, for in our commitment, we are answering the call. For this reason, we are rewarded beyond our imagination. This is the Law.

Chapter 1 - Exercise:

Do one step each day in order, without reading the next step. This is extremely important to gently begin your breakthrough.

To clearly identify your purpose, please do the questions in order. Use a separate piece of paper for each step. Feel free to take 10 minutes each day for each step. Complete them within seven consecutive days.

1. Write down a hobby, activity or work in which you get (or did get) happily lost or what just simply makes you feel downright good inside. If for any reason you have abandoned it, identify when or what was going on at the time, and why you stopped doing it. Write details. Let it out. Feel the emotion.

2. Get a separate sheet of paper. Without **any** pre-thought, write down immediately all the reasons you have not succeeded in whatever you are trying to accomplish. It is important to write this down immediately without concern of content, length, grammar, appearance, or any judgment whatsoever. This can be either a personal or a business goal. Let it flow.

3. From the list in step 2, identify the reasons that are not fear-based.

4. Write down what would help you succeed in your chosen goal.

5. Write down why you **can** succeed.

6. Read this chapter again as if the title was, *There Is No Impossible Dream*. Write down or highlight what resonates well for you after the second reading. You will hear different things this time.

7. Throw away the pages from steps 2, 3 and 4. Let them go! Replace them with the last paragraph of this chapter.

8. Your dream and life's purpose were identified in Step 1. Commit to involving yourself in it everyday for at least 15 minutes each day. Make the time! Enjoy your compliments and let them echo in your thoughts!

2

Taming
the Inner Critic

*"Experience your greatness that you have
not been told by your parents. Instinctively,
you know that you are greatness itself but
you are stifled by the suggestion of the
world, so there is a struggle within you. The
truth you instinctively know is at war with
the truth you have been conditioned to
accept." — Bro. Ishmael Tetteh*

Fear paralyzes the mind, causing us to become prisoners shackled by our own emotions. Avoidance or denial of the fear does not make it go away, but look it square in the face to bare its uselessness in this human experience called life. Although weak, fear strongly chooses failure. Once the underlying fear is identified, it can be removed to allow success as the choice in the situation.

The ego is a terrified bully masquerading as a devoted and caring friend but contradicts itself as an inner critic dictating regretful responses to people and circumstances. That persistent inner critic that says we are not good enough, pretty enough, educated enough, thin enough, rich enough, young enough or some other negative belief used to prove alleged unworthiness of pleasant desires, is the ego.

The ego arms our inner wars with seeming proof of these beliefs through its interpretation of incidences in our daily lives. These crippling beliefs are what handicap our lives from becoming what we desire.

Recognition of the ego is necessary in diffusing negative influences that prevent achieving goals, having ideal relationships, and seeing the Truth. Learn how to respond to the ego voice wherever it shows up and recognize when it is active in decision-making. See beyond its disguises and useless gifts.

Relinquishment of ego-based beliefs reveals the ego's worthlessness. Until we see its worthlessness, it is difficult to let go of the choices offered by the ego. To convince us of its worth, it appears a warrior for our well-being in feuds it creates.

Frantically, it tries to convince us that it is indeed us and is merely being supportive, especially in roles of victimization. It assures us everyone else is out to get us, destroy us, ridicule us, tarnish our reputation, or reveal our ugly secrets. Be aware of these ego interpretations for this is what imprisons us to fear.

As the ego thought system is abandoned, it fights for its life. It does not give up easy since it has countless years invested in us. The ego attempts to exhaust us with distractions to assure its continuance in our affairs and thoughts. Disguised as a security blanket, it is an insecurity blanket we have relied upon all these years.

How do we get rid of the ego? The exercises in this chapter aim at recognizing the ego, not how to get rid of it, and understand why we have given it our power. Its existence is necessary in this world, but it should not rule our choices. Free will is our gift opposite the ego, communicating as a right-guiding nurturer (inner Voice) and inner knowing.

Amidst the ego's loud cruel heckling, the encouraging Voice speaks softly. The ego vies for our undivided attention, but the Voice cannot be muted. It is a choice and right to free will. Both the ego and the Voice must exist to have free will. Together, infinite choices can be created. To have only the Voice without the ego, where is choice? Two or more from which to choose provide choice; anything less becomes something mandatory.

Choices of the ego assure chaos while choices whispered affectionately by the Voice assure peace. Our entire lives are affected by our choices. Ego choices are limited, selfish, and offer only temporary gratification. What we experience is filled with false gratification.

Whether we progress or regress in meeting goals is determined according to how much of the ego's influence we allow. It has created our belief system based on its interpretation of situations, relationships, and things. As we unlearn old beliefs, the ego tries to influence our new interpretations, shoving mounds of doubt into our thoughts when this happens. Feelings of confusion or loss are natural, but temporary.

Knowledge of our powerful Voice has been blocked because the ego has sent us in search of what it claims is now lost. Nothing is lost; we have merely forgotten.

How often do we lose our keys? They were never lost... we just forgot where we placed them. They were right where we left them, sometimes right in our hand or pocket.

Ever notice how sometimes the moment we throw up our hands and give up the search, the keys appear as if by magic? That is a moment of total release, a letting go. Blockages are removed to see clearly. Most times, *we* are not even convinced the keys were truly right before us all the time. However, time is not used analyzing our oversight. We just pick up the keys and continue the task we had set out to do. When we picked up this book, we found lost keys!

The gentle Voice has all the keys to open the doors needed to achieve all we desire. We learn to recognize and trust Its guidance. When the Voice chooses, it takes into consideration all components of life's big picture from start to finish.

With the Holy Spirit, all choices are made from Truth. When interpretations of life begin to come from Truth, nothing can permeate our peace; our whole world is redefined in joy. Response to things is guided by our Voice of inner knowing. With this wisdom, the ego voice is silenced at will, and you are back in control of your life.

Example using an artist:
You feel great every time you express your ideas on canvas. It feels wonderful. You are in heaven whenever you paint your thoughts. You become deeply absorbed in this activity that comes easy to you. How wonderful it would be to do it for a living you think but...

Ego: "Credentials are required to start your own art business. You have not taken any formal classes or training. Just because you think you paint well does not mean you can sell anything let alone make any money at it! Others are much better. See... look at that beautiful painting. You could never get that much money for yours! It's not worth it!"

Voice: "You can create things and express on canvas like no other has before. No, it is not a Picasso or Renoir; those are not art styles you like anyway. You have your own beautiful and unique style, and gee, you do it magnificently well and without any formal training!"

Everyone was created with an inner instruction manual for his or her heart's desire. Some call it a *knack* for what they do best. It is your purpose, your gift *from* God. What you do with it is your gift *to* God.

Chapter 2 - Exercise:

This exercise is preparing you to recognize the ego voice (inner critic). Recognition of the ego is the first step in reclaiming control of your life, getting what you want out of life, and achieving emotional independence.

1. Notice throughout each day this week when you compare your intellect, skills, body, or emotions to someone else. Observe it. Do nothing about it right now. Just observe.

2. Note when someone else does the same thing to him/herself.

3

What Do You Expect From God?

"Leave behind your ideas of how God should behave."— Dr. Michael Beckwith

What do you expect from God? Has He disappointed you from time to time? Did He not respond in the time, from the resource, or to the degree you expected?

Expectations tremendously affect our relationship with God. Although our faith is very difficult for Him to obtain from us and even more difficult to maintain in our lives, God has to pass our daily tests to qualify for our little faith in Him.

We attempt to first make God physical then dress Him in detail according to our extensive criteria. We arrange His hair, day and priorities. Some have seen Him or experienced Him then published that information in books we have read;

therefore, we feel we know what He looks like and how He should respond.

After an attempt to humanize Him into a super human, we impose demands on His time, perception, and response in our lives. Our limited vision and experiences thus create a limited god of high expectation. We begin to seek the created image we now call God, rather than the limitless and almighty God we originally sought.

We expect Him to answer our prayer quickly; answer it through means we think best; fulfill it without our participation; or allow us to show Him how it should be done, then He will earn our praise and belief in Him. Too often, we take the problem back from God to make sure it is resolved on time in the right way. When an acceptable resolution does not happen, we blame God for the failure. Then, there are those who do not seek Him at all.

In some cases, those in abusive relationships are more faithful to that unkind human being, who does not meet their needs, than they are to God Who will. Their lives are full of terror, pain and scattered bits of kindness. Yet, they are less afraid to depend upon this unloving person than God. Repeatedly, broken promises are given chance after chance, year after year to correct. Why not give just half that effort to God?

Although God always responds to our requests, we are not always satisfied with His idea of the answer. The amount or degree of the results disappoints us. It is not what we expected nor does it look anything close to the answer. We know how God should respond; we know all the rules, we think. Therefore, we question why He is not living up to His expected role. Surely He knows how much we need and how soon. Is he paying attention?

Some prayers become demands. When His response appears after our preferred due date; again we are not happy. "It's too late now," we claim. How could God be so slow, thoughtless, and cruel? We feel ignored and degraded, which makes us question our worth to Him.

We bring out the guilt archives and search for one we suspect may have caused God's undesired response. Something there, we are sure, has not been dealt with correctly or completely to God's satisfaction. That something is not clear and probably does not exist at all yet it tortures one's mind with fear and guilt.

Guilt is renewed and we become angry with ourselves for *missing* something, for failing to meet the requirements for atonement in some archived case. Our entry to heaven seems threatened. In fearful desperation, we seek to restore our admission status to heaven.

We create rituals and rules in our relationship with God for a prime position in this human race. Prayer time is scheduled regimentally with certain things, people, environments, reasons, and circumstances. Church services, seminars, and workshops are attended for faith renewal. Some are attended to satisfy church curriculum or religious dogma. An annual volunteer event may require some hours, one evening, or a weekend. Our offering, dress, and social conduct conform to church dogma. Hopefully, these gestures will help win approval and worthiness for the thing we ask of God.

After some time, this *dedication* becomes overwhelming. A great deal of physical and mental effort is required, which takes its toll. Guilt is stronger than before and faith becomes extremely weak because we could not endure those self-imposed commitments.

Some people even leave their church or God altogether. They are disappointed in God for all the energy put into securing an entry to heaven. The regime was created by their own imaginations, not any law of God, yet He is blamed for the seeming failure. That dedication was fear and ego-driven, guaranteed to fail.

Expect God to answer all prayers, but do not expect him to follow human or institutional rules or criteria to do it. It is best that we let go of our rules of how God should behave. Let God be God. Peace and all else we desire will manifest in our lives in a big way.

Chapter 3 - Exercise:

Write down:

1. What resources, facts, and data have you used to define your expectations of God?

2. Were you the author of that information? If not, who or what was?

3. Make a request to God with no criteria attached and watch the response unfold. Try not to alter or manipulate the outcome. Be aware of your thoughts and actions during this time.

4

Divorce and Other Separations

"We can deny Love but we cannot lose it."
— Helen Gordon

We form special relationships with people, conditions and things. When we are faced with an adverse form of separation from these special relationships, we respond with anger. The ego urges us to attack according to those images but peace cannot be defended with attack.

Special relationships support a sense of love, victimization, humility or seemingly promote our worth. The special relationship for love is used to express love, feel loved, and give love.

Being a victim may seem a strange special relationship, but it is popular. It serves to project our guilt, failure and fear onto others. Those who are chosen for this relationship are used to blame for shortcomings and failures in one's life. This is an attempt to relinquish guilt resulting from the outcome of certain choices or to justify them. Also, the relationship is used to explain unfavorable situations or circumstances.

Humility is sometimes used hand-in-hand with victimization. People chosen for this relationship provide recognition or approval to support the need to be validated or praised for being a good person or martyr. It is also a position used to crucify others with proof of justification.

No one is angry at a fact. It is always an interpretation that gives rise to a negative emotion regardless of our seeming justification by what appears to be fact. Fear is the source of this anger for we feel victimized by the separation. This adds to the difficulty to forgive.

Through fear, the ego convinces us that we will suffer an irreplaceable loss; a part of us will be ripped away, leaving us dysfunctional or incomplete. We have depended upon these relationships to fulfill those aspects that define our worth and make us whole.

Although the past no longer exists, we keep it alive through special relationships. It is best not to join it with the current one because the special relationship takes vengeance on the past. In an attempt to heal the pain of the past, the ego remains fully committed to it, ignores the present and makes it difficult to achieve the peace we seek.

No special relationship is experienced in the present. Forms of the past develop it and make it what it is. In the past, we learned to define our own needs and acquire methods for meeting them on our own terms.

The ego's use of special relationships is also fragmented. The ego seeks out certain aspects in a relationship that meet our perceived needs. It chooses one part of one aspect, which suits its purpose, while it prefers different parts of another aspect. This is a form of separation and judgment, one relationship against the other.

Such separation imposes limitations upon the special relationship, which we have created. These limitations are again defined by the past. It is impossible to let go of the past without letting go of the special relationship. Trying to apply the past to the current relationship frustrates the current partner.

This special relationship is an attempt to re-enact the past and change it. Imagined slights, remembered pain, past disappointments, perceived injustices and deprivations all find a place in the special relationship, which becomes a way in which we seek to restore our wounded self-esteem.

As we grow in wisdom, our perceptions, tolerations and values change. When a relationship no longer meets our needs as we have defined, the ego uses guilt as a means of reclaiming it as it was. Projection of this guilt has proven effective in manipulating a situation for our own benefit.

No one likes to feel guilty, so they succumb to meeting our needs. Eventually they begin to feel resentment, feel imprisoned or bound to pleasing us. By now, they have no idea what they are really reacting to through us. The interpretation is now fully distorted from its original meaning.

Retaliation seems the only escape to freedom. Attack is returned to project the guilt back to us.

Projection of guilt then becomes circular, resulting in emotional or physical scars, allowing the ego to control our minds and ruin our relationships.

Life becomes even darker through this self-created prison. However, only we hold the key to our freedom, by ceasing to attack. Attack is inspired when some need is not being met. Those needs that we wanted fulfilled were cries out to be loved. Replace attack with Love since that is really what we fear losing. We can deny Love but we cannot lose it.

Nevertheless, we went outside ourselves to seek Love, expecting to find it in a place better than God. The seeming absence of Love feels like we are unworthy of it. So, the ego says that if we are unworthy of Love then we deserve to be punished.

Self-hate through self-punishment begins to unfold, appearing in every area of our lives. It begins to be projected onto others. Others attack back to what **seems** to be projected. Opportunities for victim relationships become numerous.

The ego limits our perception of others to the body and distorts our vision of their purpose in our lives. Relinquishment of this perception lets us see the light, which radiates from others' holiness. Every relationship is a holy relationship. There is a lesson within it. When we release the wrong to see the good in all things, we release the greatest liberating power of our being.

Start by forgiving adversaries for they are not aware of what they are projecting. Look on nothing with condemnation. See only Love. The solution is not to change the person but to change our perception of the person, the relationship and as a result, the situation.

After this shift happens in the mind, forgiveness is required, which, may be difficult to do. The ego depends upon our acceptance of its perceptions for its existence. It thrives on the chaos we allow in our relationships. Forgiveness transforms the chaos to peace and reveals the truth of the matter.

The ego will become more vicious as Truth is discovered. It sees Truth as a threat to its committed existence in our lives. Take time in this transition toward Truth, for haste can give welcome to harmful ego perceptions that cause discouragement and overwhelm, damaging faith and relationships.

Relationships serve a purpose, a need, fill a void---sometimes falsely so. The ego will feed us thoughts to convince us that we cannot find a replacement anywhere else. These needs come into our lives to remind us where the source of our needs is really met. Only God can meet our valuable needs. We must always remember this lesson. Needs can sometimes be experienced through others but always remember the Source.

Many times, there is fear of abandonment, which is the ego claiming that we will be rejected and thus, alone. We do not want to be alone. But, who can truly be alone when God has accepted us.

Lessons come back in relationships until we learn them. They come back in different forms but the basic lesson does not change until learned. Sometimes people do terrible things to each other. It is the ego attacking what is not really there.

Many times the other person feels abandoned, attacked, or unloved. However, the ego is what defined these things based upon the past, society or cultural rules of sorts.

Often the relinquishment of a relationship feels like a loss but it is really a push forward to our better yet to be. Neither the past nor the future exist, only the present, but the ego will try to predict a desolate future based upon the past relationship. From this, it tries to diminish our worth.

Relationships do not define our worth nor increase it. Each person's worth is established by God; therefore, nothing is lost when forgiving someone. It is not a pardon but a release of our own self from the emotional prison often created through grudges and resentment built from the relationship.

When forgiving, we must begin with ourselves. While forgiveness of others may come quickly, relinquishment of guilt and self-forgiveness will take more time.

Chapter 4 - Exercise:

Write down:

1. What relationship would you like to get over?

2. Write in detail what you would like to tell someone you feel has offended you.

3. What would be the loss if you do not tell them?

4. What would be the gain if you do not tell them?

5. What do you want to become of the other person?

6. What do you want to become of your new life?

5

Self-Worth

"How can you allow your life to be run by opinions of people who themselves do not know why they have those opinions?"
— *Bro. Ishmael Tetteh*

Our existence is a Will of God. God does not create worthless things. He has no use or interest in valueless things. What would be the point? Each role we have accepted in the Will of God is valuable. To have a role in God's will can only be valuable.

The ego has attempted to convince us that our relationship with God has diminished; we have no worth appealing to God. It is a strong campaign to de-value us in hopes of winning our allegiance.

The Self cannot be attacked, belittled, or de-valued in any way by the ego's words, thoughts, or actions. We can only remain magnificent, powerful, and valuable.

Our Self desires to fulfill the Will of God, fears nothing of this world and remains anchored in Its oneness with God. This is who we truly are at any given instant of human time.

The Self is one's divine Spirit, housed by the physical body. It never forgets who it is as God has purposed it or its relationship with God.

The Self is real and knows only reality created by God. An attempt to alter a bit of reality will only cause true reality to disappear in our own lives. The ego's reality would then gain influence. There is nothing to gain from such a gesture since it is valueless.

Ego reality has no value. It serves no purpose, but the ego will try to deceive us by presenting forms of its reality, which appear to define its value to us or offer valueless immediate gratification. The ego will try to deceive us by offering appealing forms, which appear to define or prove value of the form that it presents.

We can always choose again. When we recognize we have accepted the ego's gift, we can choose things of value instead. It is simple to do;

however, the ego will make it appear difficult because it senses rejection of its offer and needs to keep us blind about its value.

As we reject what the ego offers, it will clutter our path to truth with piles of guilt. It will bombard us so heavily with guilt that we tire of dodging, ducking and jumping through hoops to escape this guilt we never had.

Whenever wearied of some pressing guilt, breathe slowly and deeply saying, "I decline it. This is not valuable, so it does not belong to me."

As we embody this Truth more, the ego may be granted a guest pass sometimes in our lives in periods of uncertainty but it will never have control again. It will have a very short stay.

We will watch its tricks and games. As observers, we no longer choose to participate in what is valueless, not accepting what is unnecessary in the unfoldment of our divine purpose or not inviting what interferes with our inner peace.

Put-Downs

During the holidays, family, social and business gatherings happen. The camaraderie, joking around and merriment can be enjoyable. Some conversations include put-downs meant as friendly gestures. From these put-downs, we define our self-value and determine our worth, which scars our souls more than we realize.

Bringing the comments forth to observe identifies where we may have gotten the mad idea that we are not worthy of certain things. Listen closely to these comments and observe the person saying them, even if they are our own comments. (This may require remembering an unpleasant past gathering).

Looking at those put-downs objectively as possible will help identify hidden fear, shame and insecurity. Bring them forward out of the dungeon of denial to release to the Holy Spirit. As a result, we will find that the *put-downs* will diminish with time because we will no longer attract them. Also, we will begin to understand their source or created purpose and value them less and less.

When we looked at those put-downs we found that many of them we did not believe ourselves, never have, but they have been taught to us. They are not funny any more. We picked them up from somewhere or someone else, who knows when.

Notice how sometimes the put-downs were used to *fit in* the conversation at hand, the camaraderie, or perhaps to project guilt or attention onto someone else. The ego says that if we do not fit in, then we are just a no-count unwanted wallflower. Rejection screams in our ears. Avoiding rejection becomes very important. Camaraderie feels like a welcoming. We do not want to feel left out.

When our harmless shortcomings are being played with, it becomes a threat to revealing those that must remain secret. If we can point out someone else's faults then we distract attention from our own or justify our own.

Self put-downs can often be harsher than ones from others. We are more forgiving of others shortcomings than our own. It is common for put-downs to be echoes of comments of our parents, siblings, teachers, or others long past. Because of this archive of put-downs, we can better understand why we are never upset for the reason we declare. This is an archive of insults never forgiven, never released. This corpse of put-downs negatively ignites our emotions.

Most often we are reacting to insults of the past not the issue at present or the person at present. This is also why forgiveness is necessary for often the present person is not really attacking us, but the past memory of someone's insults is stabbing murderously at our self-esteem. These put-downs, that had so much impact in the past, can be identified as *buttons* today. When they get pushed (remembered), we react as if the insults were yet real in the present (even when we are not conscious of it). Now we no longer need to accept these ego claims about us.

No longer will anyone's ego projections affect us. We can choose again to finally erase those things of the past, which do not serve us today and retrain our beliefs about ourselves. Retraining will push many buttons and identify new ones, but do not be discouraged. The buttons come forth and visible to be healed. Take a good look at them. Most buttons are in response to "what will people think?"

We think someone's opinion can actually change who we are or lessen our worth. When a person expresses an undesirable opinion about what was done, respond with, "I am confident in my actions and we can discuss it later if you would like" (set up a later time to meet with the person). When a response feels like an attack say, "What you did does not feel loving and I need to think about it." These prepared responses allow time to look within for the answers without an embarrassing reaction to later regret.

Opinions may feel like the ego has dug up a corpse of the past and dumped it into the present like toxic waste. The corpse is probably a secret where self-forgiveness has not been completed. Self-forgiveness is in order here for God has no investment in errors and is not in agreement with our misbelief about ourselves. Fortunately, our thoughts do not affect our worth, not even for an instant.

What we thought was true, is not. Now we see it differently. We must forgive ourselves since God has forgiven us; all we need to do is accept that He has. We also need to forgive others so that the guilt of the matter does not live on with us and does not push buttons in our relationships and situations that remind us of it.

Chapter 5 - Exercise:

Take more than one day to complete this exercise if necessary. Write down:

1. Identify someone you admire but do not know personally and who does not know you. Describe why you admire them.

2. What traits or habits have determined their worth in your opinion?

3. Which ones do you feel you do not have and why?

4. What can you do to obtain those traits or habits?

5. Identify two buttons you have.

6. Who pushes them?

   - Name a specific person.

   - What type of person are they?

7. What value does that person have in your life?

8. What is your response when these buttons are pushed?

9. What justifies your response?

10. How would the person identified in step 1 respond to those buttons?

6

How to Pray

Your Blessings Are Waiting For You

"...if two of you agree on earth about anything they ask, it will be done for them by my Father in heaven. For where two or three are gathered together in my name, there am I in the midst of them."
— *Matthew 18:19-20.*

We cannot possibly desire too much since we cannot imagine beyond our limited experiences. Pray for absolutely anything desired. God's gifts are inexhaustible. Scarcity and littleness are unknown in the mind of God. Prayer is our direct line to our good. It is our pure conversation with God.

Prayer of ill will not be answered since it is actually a request to either curse, judge, or punish. Revenge and karma do not need our assistance. One's own guilt will find where it **really** hurts most. We can only imagine according to our own limited experiences.

Pursuing revenge builds a strong wall of guilt, frustration, resentment and anger. We want someone to pay for what they have done, to see how wrong he or she was, and how right we were about the situation.

These things manifest as illness in our body in some form. Thus, we become mentally and physically bound by the revenge. Disease becomes evident both inwardly and outwardly.

Prayer of good will heals. The healing can be for either tangible or intangible desired blessings or both. This is our choice. Do not worry; all prayers are answered. Cast worry aside for prayers are neither ranked nor rated. They are not placed on a waiting list. God's desire is to give us the Kingdom. Our desire is His desire.

Our cup of blessings will overflow for it cannot hold all that is ours simply for the asking. Ask it in prayer. Allow the cup to fill beyond its capacity and always share what is in it to make room for more.

As we pray for whatever we desire, all events and things are set in motion to fully respond to our prayer requests. These events and things were unfolding before we even knew to ask for anything.

God does nothing special to fulfill our desires. He just takes the cups of our desires and fills them. If there is guilt in what we pray for, then our prayer may have the appearance of not being answered. Guilt is always disruptive, blocks, and serves no purpose. It asks for punishment on your behalf and finds it.

What we anticipate from feelings of guilt, that which does not yet exist, is what prevents us from freely receiving or recognizing our good. Anticipation laced with guilt produces anxiety. Anxiety attacks the mind that sickens all or part(s) of the body.

Our minds become overwhelmed by the body's malfunction. The malfunction creates more anticipation of how great the illness might be. The anxious mind will exaggerate the illness by asking, "What if I become disabled? What if I require surgery? What if this is an incurable disease?" These *What-Ifs* become increasingly exaggerated. The thoughts it creates, lead to depression.

When we are finally diagnosed with having an easily curable ailment, we are immediately released from the clutches of the ego. Doom vanishes. Truth is revealed. We are more than glad to accept our positive diagnosis and become whole once again. Exhale in joy. We fought the fight and won!

In our wholeness, we entertain the petition through prayer, but soon fearfully abandon it. The ego convinces us that we will only become sick again from the unfoldment process necessary for the blessing to completely manifest. It whispers, "This is not for you to have. You have not earned worthiness of it yet. Your healing is not real. They made a mistake!" The ego's distraction further blinds us from the Truth.

What we think is our reality, that is, sickness, is only in the mind. Let these ego thoughts pass. In reality, we cannot get sick if we choose not. Denying this reality will create sickness.

Anticipate only good and let **that** manifest! The good within us is far greater than any claimed imperfections, circumstances, or situations. Alleged imperfections reveal the ego's influence. Use it as a nudge that the thing that would teach us has been covered up. Every circumstance in our lives has come to teach us something.

Be inspired by every circumstance by seeing the opportunity it presents. Begin focusing on this good for it is powerful. Weakness, failure, nor adversity of any kind can survive this awareness or destroy its positive power in our lives.

Let a multitude of blessings enter the garden within and there plant the seeds of faith. Sow, fertilize, nourish those seeds, and then wait expectantly for good to grow from them. Harvest time comes to fill our storehouse with good to support us through the seeming harsh winters of our mind.

Seeds of faith need not be perfect or large; they only need to be as large as a mustard seed. Planting this garden lets God know we are ready to accept the gift that has always been available to us.

Faith does not knock at the door; it opens it, walks in and asks expectantly. We only need ask, that is, claim what has always been in our storehouse. Growing this faith within for our inner self gives faith power, though the outer self is charged to apply it.

Applying faith in our actions is a recognition and acknowledgment of Truth, perhaps beyond our understanding right now. Truth cannot be explained or described in words; it can only be experienced. We cannot be safe from Truth but in Truth; therefore, there is nothing to fear. Awareness of Truth will correct all erroneous perceptions of life and open our floodgates to receive unlimited good in every aspect of our lives.

God **wants** to give us all that we desire without any extra effort or begging whatsoever. No request is any more difficult or larger than another is for God; He has no such categories. Only the ego would try to place limitations on the power of God. Sacrifice gives our request no more meaning or urgency as the ego would have us believe.

With God, all things are possible. Sometimes we must allow the Holy Spirit to know this for us. We must embody it with all our heart, with all our mind, seeing ourselves no more as helpless, for the Holy Spirit lovingly awaits to assist us at a moment's notice. It loves to do what it has been purposed, to support us in creating an opening to enjoy its purpose in our lives.

Chapter 6 - Exercise:

Before you pray, go to your special place and become still and quiet.

Release any judgments or images whatsoever of yourself or others, any bad or good thoughts about anyone, any images of people or things; clear your thoughts of any preconceptions of your petition. Let it all go!

In this state of mind, you come to God as a child, in complete innocence, open mind and without judgments. Come now, pure in heart and mind with your petition, knowing that the Lord is your shepherd, you shall not want of anything at all.

Find a prayer you like and read it every day. As often as you wish, choose a new one. Your prayer can also be a daily affirmation or a simple thank you.

You are a child of God and He holds nothing against you. This is how God sees you. This is how God knows you. Expect the unexpected good. Expect a Miracle!

7

Is Your Guilt Inherited?

"All events in our lives mold us into what we are today according to our interpretation of the event."— Helen Gordon

E ver feel resentment when responding from a place of past guilt once again thrown in your face? Consciously and unconsciously, the resentfulness grows at each imposition of that response. Each imposition brings the past to the present where it is interpreted as a means of control, manipulation or punishment. Right at the time of the original incident or once we understood the consequences, we honestly felt **bad**! No one had to tell us it was a bad decision.

Perhaps in more ways than others know, we paid a dear price for it at that very moment. Contrary to the ego needs of others, endless payments of restitution are not required. No one knows how thoroughly we served our guilty sentence as intimately as we do. We paid for it in full and then some.

We were children doing childish things when our values were understandably different. We were merely seeking love, approval, or security in the best way we knew how. Observe what invited the guilty act in the first place. What was its inspiration? Was it to attack, defend or oppose someone? Once we find out what sad tears took us there, our vision can be cleared to see the path to joy again. This is the first step; allow time to *unlearn*.

Consciously or unconsciously, a great deal of guilt can be bred from parent/child or other childhood and adolescent relationship. In the case of parents, an imposed experience on their child is often times an expression of love, "It's for your own good! This hurts me more than it hurts you!" Our parents' own experiences both as adults and children along with suspicion, anticipation, or foresight often caused them to be more vulnerable to ego choices in regards to deciding for their children. So much fear influenced their child rearing decisions.

Parents fearfully tried to protect us from becoming painfully lacking in some aspect of our adult lives. Their intentions were only trying to teach that which they strongly believed would sustain us in our adult lives, that is, *raise us* correctly. If they could not prepare us as society expected and deemed correct, they were failures. Guilty! Parents avoid becoming guilty of failed parenting which could subsequently cause us (the children) pain and suffering. They wanted to be proud parents of our joy, not our pain.

Other's egos often say things that are from their own fears. Often there is no harm intended for they were not aware of their own egos speaking. Their egos convinced them they were telling us only what was good for us. Many times, it was fear **for** us. Sometimes it was fear **of** us. Other times it was deliberate attack for manipulation purposes for our own good. Yet, it was all still from their own guilt or fear. From this fear, we embodied their rules so strongly that they became our own thoughts.

The exercises in this chapter will help to unlearn fear-based rules and learn new ones to identify and release guilt; hence, change is inevitable. Change, a threat to the ego, is a forward accomplishment from an ego past. The more we learn about the ego, the more we learn it is unreliable, deceitful, and destructive. It will no longer be desired as we recognize it offers nothing good.

As we unlearn, the ego may try to influence our interpretation of what we are learning. It will fight for its life since it has invested all it has in us. This will make the unlearning process seemingly challenging at times, creating an inner war. However, God's will is that we win. Winning is certain through releasing and discarding issues, people, and perceptions of the past. It is an exchange of an ugly past for a beautiful present.

The ego cannot tolerate release from the past for its life, its very existence, is there. Although the past is gone forever, the ego tries to preserve its image by responding as if the past **is** the present. It dictates our reactions to those we meet in the present from a past reference point, obscuring our present reality.

This chapter is **not** trying to teach how to forget an incident; it is aiding to help see it differently so that the healing process can begin. The mind does not forget. That is the law of memory. By seeing the incident differently, it will no longer have **any** affect on our lives or emotions. We will be able to see the uselessness of guilt; perhaps even see other areas of our lives affected by it, especially health and relationships. Then we can replace it with peace. Yes, peace can exist in that same space. It has always been there waiting to be revealed.

Guilt is the ego's way of imprisoning us in the past where it can control us. That is the only place the ego can exist. Its existence depends upon the past, which no longer exists; therefore, what no longer exists cannot possibly be real. The ego will lead us to the past, convince us that is happening now to make it real in the present

Often referred to as recollection of the past, we experience it frequently as a reoccurring nightmare or waking up in a cold sweat, not completely understanding the terror. When allowed, emotions, visions, and people of the past unite within our conscious mind to offer again a past experience, which now only exists in thought. This re-creation then becomes accepted as "fact" of our guilt then manifests as disease in our bodies.

It cannot be real and it is merely an illusion struggling to be real. Once the ego has convinced us of the realness of the past; then Truth, which is truly real, becomes more difficult to accept. Reality is then seen as the impossible illusion.

Begin to realize the truth that we are greater than any circumstance, alleged failure, or illness. Whenever our Spirit welcomes Truth, our ego feels attacked and so strengthens guilt through emotional re-enactments of the past as an attempt to purge this Truth from our mind. Truth cannot be purged but may have that illusion when repressed with stacks of guilt accepted from the ego.

Good is always ready and willing to come forth when we ourselves are open to receiving it. The good in us is far greater and more powerful than any issue outside of us. Giving energy to that good actually magnifies the good in, through and around us. We meet with the good before anything else. It reveals the insignificance of the undesirable, where the undesirable decreases moment by moment to nothing, which it has always been. We recognize how those things were stepping-stones to our greater yet to be, to inspire our purpose.

Release those beliefs that contradict well-being. To do so is to acknowledge the spiritual. It is through the spiritual knowledge where the mental and physical are made whole and complete. We can choose to exercise this free will to establish our own interpretation at any time.

Remain in the Truth that we are fully loved and forgiven by God. This is the lesson. This is the message of God. For in God's eyes, we are worth it!

God has established our worth anyway. And that is what prevails. It is the pure truth about us. Our worthiness is real. Any judgment otherwise is simply an illusion of the ego fighting to be real.

Chapter 7 - Exercise:

Write down:

1. List things you have heard a relative of a previous generation speak of in relation to guilt.

2. What did you hear nearly daily or very often with the word, *guilt,* in the same sentence while growing up?

3. What similar things do you, your siblings or friends define as something worthy of guilt?

4. What does your religious practice define as something to feel guilty about? Do you agree? Why or why not?

5. Where do you find the guilts identified in steps 3 and 4 in your life?

6. Have you personalized them or imposed them on others?

8

Stop Recycling Guilt

*"They whose guilt within their bosom lies,
imagine every eye beholds their blame."*
—- Shakespeare

Being an unconscious emotion most of the time, guilt can be very deceiving. Guilt is merely an error in thinking in need of correction, nothing more. Since the purpose of guilt is pain, obedience to it is therefore painful. Guilt seeks any form of pain be it physical or mental and draws it to its owner. It has many disguises hidden in relationship conflicts, parent/child conflicts, career frustration, low self-esteem, unworthiness, fear, failure and disease. The mind is terrified to uncover the reason for the guilt for fear of what it might reveal.

Once guilt is brought forth, it can be released for correction. Releasing guilt unlocks our mind's prison doors for us to emerge into a world of peace that awaits our coming. The ego wants us to believe we are creating a prison if we release guilt rather than freedom. Therefore, only the ego is an obstacle to peace. It projects itself into our interpretation of challenges such as confrontation, insecurity, and doubt so it can easily produce more guilt for us.

Continue the journey beyond the veil of guilt to Love, where guilt ends. Love and guilt cannot abide in the same home (the mind) simultaneously. Also, only one can be obeyed at a time.

Surely, our allegiance to the ego will be weakened if in our commitment we attempt to discard guilt. With its own agenda, the ego appears supportive in this attempt. Readily, the ego creates even more guilt to discard. The ego's means of discarding guilt slyly requires guilt-filled activity.

Guilt is blinding and futile. So much energy is put toward relinquishing guilt that the good we do often goes unnoticed. The only thing we remember is our useless battle to get rid of it. Endless attempts are made to correct the error. Some of the attempts are subtle ways of denying the imagined enormity of the error. Only the ego tries to create enormous influence and control over our lives.

Attempts at correction seem to heighten the guilt. The appearance of the negative results is meant to portray God as weak. If the ego can convince us God is too weak to prevent its control then it wins our commitment to depend on its tools to correct its insane creations. Unfortunately, these tools only create even more errors to undo. We end up in the ego's *seek but do not find* mode. God is not weak, He just allows choice. He does not force Himself upon anyone. Thus, correction only enters where it is welcomed.

The ego maliciously searches our lives with a fine-toothed comb, revisiting our every thought to find **anything** it can use to condemn us. In the process of making it homeless and irrelevant, through truly releasing guilt, various forms of this maliciousness arise.

Why would we expect the ego to be cooperative? Its goal is to prove the guilt it has charged us with is true. What benefit is it to accept the ego's disguised gifts as guilt? Anger, confusion, illness, and other forms of fear are what it has to offer as bonuses.

Another ego gift is the notion that more is better for us lest we lose. Excessive needs for such things as drugs (legal, illegal, nicotine, alcohol), food, spending (gambling, shopping), sex, money, sacrifice (giving, doing without), work, and exercise claim our loyalty. Each one justifies the other, allowing us to deny guilt through preoccupation with these excesses or through the escape they can falsely provide. Some excesses are justified as promoting health, success, or fun. As we become more aware of the worthlessness of these gifts, we seek peace instead.

Recognition of guilt reveals a path to peace. By choice, we have chosen this journey to peace. We have come this far safely only by the guidance of the Voice. The Voice remains available and eagerly willing to gently carry us through these times.

Chapter 8 – Exercise:

Write down:

1. Identify a reoccurring thought, which renews guilt for something that happened in your past.

2. What triggers the thought?

3. How has it interfered in your family, business or intimate relationships?

4. What is the value of holding on to this guilt?

5. Are you ready to let it go?

9

Are You Worth It?

"Expectations hurt both the one who created them and the one who tries to meet them. For each one, it is used to validate self-worth." — Helen Gordon

What do we expect of our mate, children, or parents? What do we expect of our boss, neighbor, or friend? What do we expect of ourselves? Can we live up to the expectations we have of others, from others or to ourselves? Is it worth it?

It is difficult to live up to our own and often rigorous expectations of others. Some are fantasies intended to correct the past, prove a point, or boost self-worth. These intentions are unreachable this way. When these kinds of expectations are seemingly met, there is no sense of satisfaction or accomplishment, just an empty feeling. It still feels like *unfinished business* of the past.

The past is a period, which can only be visited again in thought. The past is given superficial life from which responses are made in the present, yet the past cannot be changed regardless of the effort put into it. What is needed is a change in behavior toward life's present issues in a manner that does not attempt to re-create the past. This prevents creating new expectations or redefining the current ones.

It is very stressful and awkward to meet the expectations of someone else. For a mate, the role has many expectations defined even before the union without regard to cultural, social, religious, or family values of the other partner. Some expectations may vary by season, mood, or health. Each mate earnestly tries to make adjustments to live up to those expectations that appease the other.

Inner conflicts arise in the mate when there are differences in values from upbringing. A sense of betrayal or shame may surface when expectations go against their in-bred values. There may be fear that meeting those conflicting expectations might be spiritually or morally harmful. Inner struggles begin to happen and panic is invoked. The battle begins between mates to defend their values.

Expectations having family root origins are reflected in expectations demanded of our children. Children are given chores and responsibilities with expectations highly influenced by the parents' own childhood skills or shortcomings. For example, if the parent was challenged by math, the child either may be expected to excel in the subject or is sympathetically excused for failure in it.

Parents often attempt to heal their childhood through their children. Our parents did the same but with their own set of rules or reasons we often disliked, yet we feel ours are different, fairer, or compliment the era.

When children fail to meet these expectations, it leaves a sense of failure and feelings of inadequacy just as our parents experienced with us. Parental expectations may negatively affect parent/child relationships even for adult children. Adults sometime continue trying to fulfill these expectations given when they were children or make up for them, damaging their self-esteem. The attachment to the old expectation continues.

Parents are expected to age but not get old or have disabilities. Parents are expected to always be there for us when we need them, yet they are expected to respect our independence. Emotional support is also expected of our parents when life threatens our sanity, but they should not worry about our situation since we are adults.

It is not easy on a parent to fall short of providing what their children think they need regardless of age. It breaks a parent's heart to fail a child. No one likes to fail. Here we have the parent fearing failure and the child fearing failure. Neither wants to fail the other.

Expectations hurt both the one who created them and the one who tries to meet them. For each one, it is used to validate self-worth. When expectations require sacrifice of the other person and they meet those expectations, the recipient perceives it as an acknowledgment of their worth.

Meeting expectations wins acceptance we think, which is also used to validate self worth. Having our expectations met by someone provides a feeling of elevated worth. How much we are valued is tested. However, neither role proves nor establishes our worth. Anyone's criteria, test, or declaration does not determine our worth.

Since God declared us as precious in His sight, our worth cannot be reduced, raised, or damaged. Our precious worth can be forgotten but it cannot be destroyed; it can be perceived differently, but it cannot be changed to worse; it can be denied, but it will always be maximal. At times, it may appear re-defined by others, which can only occur in thought. Those thoughts can be accepted as true but cannot change Truth. Nothing can.

What is true for every child of God, without exception, is that absolutely everyone is worthy of being fully embraced in warm unconditional Love. God loves everyone equally and unconditionally void of any influence of our dogmas or opinions.

His love is not something we must sacrifice to get; something we must earn; or something we can purchase; it belongs to us already. Never will we be without it.

We are worth the world and God gave it to us to enjoy.

Chapter 9 - Exercise:

Write down:

1. Describe what you think is valuable about yourself that others do not seem to recognize.

2. Why is it you think they do not recognize your worth?

3. What do you base your worth on?

4. Is this basis something you adopted from an outside source or is it one you created?

5. Perhaps you have worked on a successful project under a project lead or manager. As a leader or boss, what do you expect of your team or staff that was influenced by your experience in working for that lead person or manager?

6. What are your thoughts when you are being ignored? Provide an exhaustive answer to this question.

10

Your Relationship With Yourself

"He is able to do exceedingly, abundantly above all that we ask or think, according to the power that works in us."
— *Ephesians 3:20*

Ignorance is no longer an acceptable excuse for our failures since most limitation is self-imposed. In time, we become aware of being a minute expression of the creator of all things and as such, have no limitations except those accepted in our own mind.

A spiritual goal is reachable and God has given us the tools and means to reach it. This is His will; therefore, the goal is possible. Reaching the goal is part of the journey home. God rejoices at every step that leads us nearer to Him. The closer we are, the clearer we recognize the error in our thinking and are able to release it.

This is salvation, salvation from the erred thought and resultant response. The more we accept salvation, the more we reach ourselves, and the more we remember who we are.

It is impossible not to reach ourselves since we cannot be separate from ourselves though we can fragment it in our mind. We must allow the Holy Spirit (the Voice), who is also not separate from us, to help us remember our eternal connection. Regardless of the distance it seems between God and our being, we can never separate ourselves from Him.

Acknowledging this truth helps to see who we are as God created us to be. God loves what He has created. Regardless of what we have ever done or ever said, God's perception of us remains pure, seeing only our innocence. He did not forget our innocence just because we did.

Many times on this path to our goal lies fear of damage to our self-image or self-worth. What we want people to think about us is threatened as well as the love or approval we feel we earned.

Address the fear and look at it objectively from the inside out. What we find is that there is yet value held for our "old self" and its superficial needs. Fortunately, it will pass. We will begin to like who we are, not what we created.

Do not be disappointed. We cannot regress or lose any steps toward the goal. We are yet moving forward regardless of the set back this fear seems to have caused.

Fears present only temporary delays to the next step. These delays do not erase the progress we have made so far. It is merely a pause we have taken to grieve the death of our old self as our true Self emerges.

Through pettiness, the ego exerts a great deal of chaos in our lives to convince us that control of our own lives is beyond our power. Surrendering to this thinking is useless since neither people nor things can control us without our permission.

We are yet making progress in this process and in our spiritual growth. That cannot change. We cannot regress to who we were when we started reading this book. Impossible. We will never forget what we have learned and the ego will always be recognizable now.

Our memory is continuously expanding; we cannot forget anymore. With the intentions of enticing us to forget, the ego will now try to exert guilt. It will offer guilt any opportunity it can. Recognize that only we hold the vicious guilt against ourselves by accepting it. Only we hold such malevolent thoughts in our mind accepted from the ego. Being only in our minds, these thoughts are not reality.

The ego cannot know who we are since it has no knowledge of reality. It is afraid of this stranger. In defense, it offers illusions (ego reality) to protect itself. Any threat of reality, that is, anything replacing the ego's illusion, is attacked.

Illusion sustains the ego's very existence. Illusion is its nourishment. The ego attacks thoughts to bring about more illusions, and thus renews our

73

loyalty to it. It hates rejection. Our human self projects that hate often through attacks on the body (illness), alleged bad luck, forms of victimization, or emotional stress (heart disease, hypertension, strokes, etc.). Now that we have created problems, big, small, and complex, we are terrified that God will not undo what we have created.

These problems we call mountains but they are but tiny pebbles upon the earth as far as God is concerned. There is no size or complexity to the problems we think we have. God uses no more power to fix complex problems as he does with simple ones. They are merely errors to be corrected through our perception and acceptance of the healing that awaits us.

The Atonement was offered to relinquish this self-hate for errors that have occurred in the past or will occur in the future. Christ unconditionally accepted the Atonement for us, and then sent the Holy Spirit to always be here for us. That will never change. Relax. No one is ever alone.

The Holy Spirit is always with us for guidance and strength. Our frustration may take our vision off the Holy Spirit for a moment; however, just because we look another way, does not make Him disappear.

When we get disconnected from a telephone call, we do not go anywhere. We are still where we were when we were connected. We are still who we are. Disconnections do not transport us to another country nor do we cease to exist, and the reconnection is simple.

Choose again as the Voice directs. Choose reality, which has the peace, joy and happiness we have always desired. There is no scarcity in the things we desire. There is no qualifying. There is no deadline or expiration date. The clock is not ticking away toward the last minute that we can accept these things.

Opportunity is always at hand for us to choose again. All that is ours is waiting for us. All we need has been given to us. We need only accept it.

Begin to reject the offerings of the ego, no matter how beautiful the gifts appear. Its gifts are lethal daggers to the heart laced with disease and pain.

Our blessings and peace of mind are waiting patiently for our acceptance because we are worth it. If it were not so, God would not have sent a Comforter and Guide. A child of God is eternal, precious, and priceless. We are unconditionally loved forever.

Chapter 10 - Exercise:

When you encounter a situation, where the ego attacks and is in seeming control, breathe deep, and then excuse yourself.

1. Go to a bathroom or a quiet place at work or home.

2. Ask, "What do I fear?"

3. What do you feel is being attacked? (The first response will be the ego's answer, which is usually, "I don't know.").

4. To that response ask, "Why is that important?"

5. And to that response, ask again, "Why is **that** important?"

6. Do steps 4 and 5 again, and then go on to step 7.

7. Where have you placed value? Determine if it is ego value or something of real value.

8. Why do you value this thing you think is so important?

9. Is it **your** value or one you have learned?

You will begin to recognize your own fear and discomfort. Now you are ready to give an intelligent response that is not from fear.

11

Your True Innocence

"More validity is given to how man has defined our worthiness rather than God's acceptance of us just the way we are. We weary ourselves at times trying to meet man's criteria of our worthiness for our desires by laboring to live up to man's expectations." — Helen Gordon

We learned a most unnatural habit, not communicating with our Creator. As absurd as it is, we really believe that we could indeed create such an isolation or separation from God.

Often we depend upon ourselves or our assets (bank account, career, friends, family) to see us through certain circumstances, claiming that we do not want to bother God with such pettiness. We boast about being far above making petty requests!

We rank and rate which problem to give to God. Often that changes according to the anxiety level, as a result of trying to *fix it* ourselves. The threat of devastating failure in resolving the issue sends us frantically to God.

The first miracle principle of *A Course In Miracles* declares that regardless of our requests, there is no order of difficulties for God. They are all the same. It takes no more effort for God to give us a mansion as it does a one-bedroom apartment. For him, it is just a need or desire easily fulfilled. Only the ego measures, rates, and ranks anything. God has no limitations whatsoever and His abilities are certainly not governed by the ego's criteria.

Limitations are subtly taught to us. Our limited thinking is defined by some mandated criteria of *worthiness*. Also, we put a price on our worthiness to determine if we are qualified for our desires or if we have retained our innocence. If we pay enough for it, we feel we have earned it. Payment is made in so many different ways according to the religious dogma from which we were raised as children.

Some desires we feel are granted according to how well we satisfy cultural, social or man-made laws. We accept them as valid in our lives, what we have *agreed* upon.

More validity is given to how man has defined our worthiness rather than God's acceptance of us just the way we are. We weary ourselves at times trying to meet man's criteria of our worthiness for our desires by laboring to live up to man's expectations.

The ego gets even trickier. It raises the level of these criteria using ego interpretations, and then challenges us to meet them. Although it is impossible nonsense, we condemn and crucify ourselves for failing to perfect our lives around these embellished criteria. To cover up this failure, we often seek cosmetic, career, and material goods to *prove* that we are indeed worthy of our good and really have not failed in meeting the requirements.

On the other hand, we may seek self-sabotage or place blame outside ourselves to prove that the failure was not on our account. It is a false relinquishment of responsibility where we attempt to project the outcome onto someone else in the event it is negative. Victimization works perfectly for this proof and preserves our innocence we think. Many sympathizers (usually others who are doing the same thing) support us lest they condemn and expose themselves too.

The world is just trying to make a mockery of us and pick on us unfairly we declare. We try to convince the world that our failure is not our fault. The ego has now distracted us tremendously. Focus is now on alleged failure to meet man-made and self-made criteria.

We no longer recognize that we have denied God's criteria of our innocence and that we have already met it without anyone's blessing, ritual or rule. It is impossible to meet man-made criteria consistently or perfectly, but is effortless to meet God's criteria. God's desire is merely that we remember and *accept* our innocence.

Any human being, organization, or man-made law does not determine our true innocence. Parents, siblings, friends, strangers, and children are not appointed by God to advise Him of the opinion He should hold of us. God has no use for this limited perception. The ego may insist God needs assistance, but that would be absurd.

It is exhausting to please the ego because it offers the impossible to us. It offers gifts where attainment of it neither has been defined nor exists. Criteria change daily and case-by-case because the ego does not even know its own direction or goal.

The ego offers an excuse for the change that seems so legitimate that we accept it as *fair* or necessary to reach this unknown goal. It has us chasing a goal of no definition. If there are no criteria that mark the end or fulfillment of the goal, how will we ever attain it? What is there to attain?

The exhaustion experienced by trying to reach something without an ending or existence is often expressed as a nervous breakdown, clinical depression, stress-related disease, eating disorder, spousal combat, conflicting relationship, etc.

This is not our desire, and we no longer accept it. Instead, we choose wholeness, peace of mind, prosperity, love and the eternal joy of life. These gifts of God are at hand for which we give full gratitude. Clarity is the order of each day to see and enjoy these gifts that are ours to keep, share and multiply. There is plenty. Our cups are forever full.

Chapter 11 - Exercise:

Write down:

1. What innocence do you feel you have lost?

2. What are your feelings about that loss?

3. Do you feel it is recoverable or has been restored? Why? Why not?

4. Was your innocence really lost?

5. Offer any feelings of loss to the Holy Spirit. Let Him take care of it the way that is best for you. If you find the ego becoming impatient or judging this approach, ignore it as best you can, knowing that this response is indeed for your highest good.

12

Mending the Hurt

*"What makes the pain continue is using the
ego's weak glue to put it all back together as
an attempt to reclaim wholeness."*
— Helen Gordon

The Holy Spirit mends our hearts and minds, that is, allows us to see through the eyes of Truth of how our wholeness was never shattered. In spite of the painful emotional experiences where things seem to fall apart, we remain whole, perfect, and complete. Fragmentation of our wholeness exists only in our minds. The Truth remains, we are always whole.

What makes the pain continue is using the ego's weak glue to put it all back together as an attempt to reclaim wholeness. The ego has invested tremendously in making sure we break our own hearts and blame it on someone else to disguise the source of our heartbreak.

Blame is one of its weapons against us, which shatters all types of relationships in our lives. The ego takes all those shattered pieces and glues them weakly together with an epoxy of pain, to be sure we do not forget what *they did to us*.

This is how the ego keeps us in painful situations. We stock up on layers of renewed painful memories. Nevertheless, we have learned where guilt comes from. We think that emerging from them will be sad, but actually, we emerge in joy and see how sad it was to remain in the past.

So if someone has hurt us in the past, but we have forgiven him or her, why does the memory of the instance still hurt? Does that mean we really have not completely forgiven even though we truly think we have?

True. Anything no longer real for us cannot hurt us. We keep the past hurt real in the present only in thought. If we hold on to the past, it becomes an extension of our present. The pain can only exist in thought now because the incident no longer exists. The past is gone forever although our human self may deny it by turning it into a present grudge.

Allow the Holy Spirit to dominate the human self because It does not entertain the grudge as the ego does. The ego uses the grudge as a yoke of burden and punishment for the one we claimed to have hurt us. A grudge is the ego's life sentencing of its victim; however, the sentence cannot be enforced.

Those who accept this verdict (which is purely voluntary) indeed place themselves in an emotional prison. From this prison, we will blame others for the affects of having accepted the sentence as if it were valid. Our acceptance of this sentencing is valuable to the ego because it then has us under better control.

At any time, we may dismiss the sentencing for any reason since we are our own judge. Once it is dismissed, the ego will search feverishly for guilt. There will be offers of guilt regardless of our decision.

The guilt will be from the ego's questions such as, "Why did I choose him or her? Why didn't I let go earlier? How could I be such a fool? Why me?"

The inner critic will aggressively position itself to answer these questions first in an attempt to drown out our divine inner Voice. Revoke the ego's permission to speak. Mute the inner critic by inviting the Voice to speak. Both cannot speak simultaneously because the ego is powerless. It must wait for our permission.

The Answer identifies each one's role in the lesson that was experienced as heartbreak. As ridiculous as it may sound, even this relationship was holy. Perhaps we found a strength we never knew we had. Finding it probably required a hidden talent that had been severely de-valued by the ego. Answers can reveal how a relationship was indeed a response to a prayer request. How could that be?

Say I have been a workaholic and have begun to see health debilitating signs from it. My inner Voice tells me to include more recreational activities in my life. I pray for a change to improve my health then soon meet someone and start a relationship.

I go places I had planned to go but never seem to have the time. I venture out and do things I had never done before. This new person was my inspiration, my jump-start and answer to my prayer.

Like training wheels, this person functioned to train me to develop this new activity until I was capable of doing it on my own. The support role I had created for this person crumbled at my success and readiness. It was time to be on my own.

This relationship showed me what I had been missing. My inner critic made it difficult to see how I was now better prepared.

How do we know always that what we hear is the Holy Spirit and not some ego voice or whatever? Observe. The results clarify it.

At first, just observe. We will be able to discern the ego voice from the Voice by following our instincts no matter how afraid we are. We will be able to discern our decisions of fear from our decisions of Truth. It takes practice listening to our Internal Teacher (the Voice) and to trust that power and knowingness within us.

Next time, our decision will be a better one by far, because we chose to go to the Voice with our questions. Now, we are ready to listen to the Answer. We have all the Answers; we have access to what we need. We are awesomely made. We need only accept it, believe it, and do it.

Only right now does our intuition seem frail. Listen to the Holy Spirit for guidance, and then trust what it says. The ego will throw in doubt regardless of the decision. Hold fast to the Truth of the Voice.

This does not always answer our question, but it directs us **to** the Answer within our own mind. We can accept it even if we cannot do it right now. Acceptance of it is not always easy, but necessary.

Chapter 12 - Exercise:

Write down:

1. How do you feel when you think about a heart-breaking event of your past or present?

2. How do you feel when you are not thinking about it?

3. While in the midst of an undesired emotional situation, have a conversation with yourself. Ask:

   - What do I feel is going to happen?

   - Why do I think that this could happen?

   - Is this what I **hope** will not happen?

   - If it were to happen, is this what you want on some level but afraid? Is it really the best thing for you?

   - Decide that something better is out there for you and go for it because you are worth it.

13

Your Imagined Secrets

"Denial withholds love and splits unions. It is a fabricated innocence, the keeper of secret thoughts, beliefs, and self-condemnations." — Helen Gordon

D enial is a fabricated innocence, the keeper of secret thoughts, beliefs, and self-condemnations. It pretends to know nothing of a particular situation or belief. The situation is declared unknown, non-existent. How can something denied be an unknown and how can nothing be denied? It is clearly understood on a different level since there is no way to deny something **not** known or is non-existent. What would be the point? What a silly declaration. However, our inner critic created this tool

The need for denial is to pretend the thing does not exist so it will go away without us having confrontation or admitting ownership.

91

Denial is also used to avoid responsibility of one's created world. Blame for how life has turned out is substantiated and supported through denial. Additionally, it serves as a pardon to what is interpreted as less than desirable choices.

Thoughts, responses, and outcomes from denial have to be seen for what they really are, useless, desperate, and unloving. This realization invites a threat to what was presented for others to believe about our innocence. The fear is that the victimizer's innocence will be revealed if the denial is removed. Surely all the embarrassing secrets will be exposed if the alleged victimizer is found innocent. The world will know who we really think we are which is not appealing in our opinion. The true self is feared, denied, and thus declared the facade.

There is value in denial for it also allows us to deny our imagined sentencing to punishment from God. The hope is that if we can avoid admitting we deserve the punishment, we escape the wrath of God altogether.

The thought of punishment from God is absolutely terrifying. If there is to be punishment, we want to be in control of it. As long as we can punish ourselves, we believe it may possibly satisfy God. Self-punishment is then used to bargain for a pardon of the imagined judgment we have on "the books." But the judgment happened only in our minds and God is not angry at our fantasy.

Often the fantasy is taken beyond thought to share with others. Each person feeds off the other's denial and projections. "See what they have done to me. I cannot live righteously with this abuse. I cannot possibly receive the Love of God with their vicious interference. They are keeping love away from me by treating me this way. So, you see, it is not my fault that God does not love me and punishes me with a rotten life. Why can't He see I did not do anything wrong?"

Well, this is correct, we did nothing wrong, yet it still lingers in our mind. God indeed sees only innocence in His children, although we do not acknowledge our own innocence. The mad idea that innocence cannot be restored is denying a loving relationship with God. The grieving mind denies its

93

innocence, obliterating it with desperate attempts to *fix* things on its own terms using blame and denial as its tools.

Denial is a decision to forget. Forgetting will create a journey without a purpose, forever seeking the innocence denied by guilt. Eventually things are forgotten beyond recall and profoundly lost in alleged victimization through other issues. Through these issues, we present a case to a superficial jury to prove our innocence. We hope that even God will be convinced that others were the cause of our imperfections and thus allow us entry through the gates of heaven. For reprieve, we hope God's wrath will be turned toward more deserving individuals, namely those we claim as our victimizers.

This jury will see the victimizer's guilt. Certainly God will see it too, the ego rambles. From this, the ego attempts to create in one's mind an even further separation between the victimizer and God. However, if God were to decide against anyone, He would be denying Himself. This will not happen to a child of God.

God is not seeking condemnation of His children; He is seeking their heart. God does not love one child more than another. They are all precious in His sight. He wants all of his children peacefully together even when the ego seeks further separation of them through denial.

This is the ego trying to degrade God as if God would accept what the ego has declared to be true. Since God seems to have missed the degradation, the ego presents the charge as truth for judgment. That the ego could possibly see a truth, where God could not all this time is mere arrogance of the ego.

Denial takes away and that feels powerful. Denial has no power in itself. The limitless mind can however grant power as it chooses. We cannot exclude ourselves from our mind's thoughts. Wherever we go, the thoughts will follow.

Escape from these thoughts is often sought through drugs, alcohol, sex, or other obsessions believed to grant more control. The escape is quite brief and most times is neither complete nor enjoyable. Attempts to make the escape last longer become addictions. It was never enjoyable and the addiction proves it. This is another denial to face.

None of these escape elements can save anyone; none can give peace. They only create more things to deny. Over time, the mind reaches a limit on the amount of denial it can store. The mind seeks relief for the sake of its sanity. It tires of trying to maintain a separation from God.

Nothing outside ourselves can hurt us, disturb our inner peace or be upsetting in any way. Understanding this becomes a turning point. Denial loses its value. Anger toward others is reduced or released; sickness and disease become curable; and a sense of threat is lessened proportionately. Space has now been created for love to enter, which is power. Through love, all needs are provided.

Whatever is repressed (or denied) will find a victim. The body is victimized in the form of sickness or disease. Others are victimized by this illness in various forms that make demands and generate guilt. When denial ceases, forgiveness can take its place. Forgiveness yields to total healing.

The ego does not want anyone to have knowledge of these forms. Knowledge becomes the awareness of totality, revealing the fragments of deception the ego has patched together to create the seeming totality of our lives. The ego will work tirelessly to deny this knowledge. Revelation and acceptance of this new knowledge voids the ego's existence.

Chapter 13 - Exercise:

Write down:

1. What do you **know** you have been denying?
2. What have you been told you are denying?
3. Find the similarities between them (if you had an answer to both questions above).
4. How is this denial supporting your public image?
5. How is this denial supporting your relationship with yourself?

14

Resolving Problems

"That I exert the light of love as God meant it to be. Instrument of peace, this is everyone's destiny found at the core of all religions and philosophies of life. It is a good deal better to 'be' the message than it is to tell it."

"It is not fate but yourself you are facing now."— Fenwicke Holmes.

When we do not know there is a problem to be resolved, this presents an extremely challenging situation, close to impossible to be solved. Once we acknowledge there is a problem even if we do not know what the problem is, small efforts toward revealing it will open a path of resolution. Acknowledging a problem can take some work initially, but once done, it becomes easier to do again.

The *illusion* of a problem becomes very powerful at times. The illusion exists when we either do not know consciously that there is a problem yet or denial has obliterated it.

Sometimes we exert so much effort toward resolving the **response** to the source of the problem, that we think we have in fact resolved the problem itself. What a surprise when the problem we thought was resolved re-appears. The problem was really only pushed further down into the dungeons of denial. Too often through denial, we commence with an ego resolution in places that are guaranteed not to accomplish anything.

For example, being overweight is generally a byproduct of habits such as eating too much and a high caloric intake. These habits are the response to the source of the problem. Dieting will only resolve the overeating *response* to some more deeply seeded issue. The person becomes thinner yet the real problem has not been addressed. If the eating disorder is not resolved, the next level of the overweight issue becomes diabetes, heart disease, back problems, depression, self-hatred, etc. Eventually, the excess weight comes back.

So much attention is given to the diagnosis of these additional byproducts that the issue is buried even deeper, ignored, or dismissed. Ailments affect marriages, careers, self-esteem, and life styles. It becomes a subtle but highly destructive epidemic in all areas of life. Situations, things, and people are blamed, and thus complicate the healing process.

We know when we are overweight or are over eating. No one really needs to confirm it for us. We are very aware of it. But we must remain focused on the problem, not the byproduct lest it lead to alcohol, sex, or drug abuse.

Seeking to resolve the problem through food, drugs, alcohol or sex give us the illusion of control. It is followed by feelings of failure and guilt to resolve the *real* problem. Eagerly the ego continues to lead us on the wrong path of resolution through these illusions reinforced by guilt. As long as the illusions are accepted, we have no reason to try anything else.

Life eventually seems out of control. Control has not been lost, just denied. The more these illusions are discarded, the easier it is to see that control has not changed. Control does not mean the ability to manipulate; it is the acknowledgment that

God's Will is not in opposition with our will, for any reason, at any time.

We are in full control of our lives. Dieting will not resolve the problem, acceptance that we are in control will. The seeming lack of control has birthed many of our problems since childhood. This is expressed as rebellion. Although we do not know the answer to the problem, we have already decided to reject it regardless.

When we find that we know the Answer but are yet not sure of the problem, then our knowledge is one of intellect only. Once we recognize the real problem, and then apply the Answer, we solve the real problem.

We must go beyond our thought systems, that is, inquire of the Holy Spirit, for the Answer. Miracle Principle #4 in A Course In Miracles says, "...*His Voice will direct you very specifically. You will be told all you need to know.*" [1] We need but accept the Answer, embody It, believe It, and let It resolve the problem.

The Holy Spirit goes to the source of the problem to solve it. We never resolve the problem directly, it is resolved through us, someone, or something, for the Holy Spirit always provides us with the conduit for the resolution.

Resolution first begins in our minds and from there it is made manifest by our faith. The pain is replaced with peace. Do not judge yourself as worthy of the resolution or not for as we believe, it will be given unto us. If we believe that we are unworthy of peace in the matter, as the ego would have us believe, then the madness will viciously continue.

The Holy Spirit does not judge the source of the issue, its victims, or us. Its purpose is simply to undo it and grant us permanent peace with it. We cannot take it back but we can deny the peace later and respond as if the problem were real again. The Course says, "*What you accept into your mind does not really change it.*" [2] If we did not think we deserved peace, we would not seek it. We seek what we believe.

Faith is the key and secret to obtaining what we seek. Faith pays no attention to appearances of any kind. It works upon principle that whatever we desire to accomplish, we have the power to do. Faith sees beyond physical sight to see things as they are. To have faith is to enter that place of unlimited possibilities.

Chapter 14 - Exercise:

Write down:

1. Identify a problem where you think you need more information or support to resolve it.

2. List the information and support needed such as names of people, tools and conditions.

3. List how you can obtain at least one of the items identified in step 2.

4. Prepare a resolution plan where step 1 of this plan starts with you.

    a. How important to me is it to resolve the problem? What are the benefits?

    b. What behavior do I need to change to take away some of the conflict?

    c. What thoughts can I change?

    d. What tasks need to be done? By when?

    e. What approach, tools, and people are needed to complete these tasks?

It is more important to resolve the issue than to "save face" because it can be very emotionally or financially expensive and can become a lifetime annoyance. Start by resolving it in your mind first.

15

The Secret Behind Anger

"Harboring resentments and unforgiveness is like drinking rat poison and then waiting for the rat to die." — Annie Lamott

We are the rulers of our minds, inviting what we choose. We must accept the responsibility of our own anger. However, we tend to accuse others for causing our anger as if we had absolutely nothing to do with it; if it were not for the other person, we would not be angry. This person has given us a reason to respond negatively, to defend our worth, our values, or our reputation as far as we are concerned.

Substitute yourself in the following dialogue example of the subconscious process of anger:

Beginning of dialogue:

Since you have attacked me then I must attack you. You leave me no choice. I would not need to attack you if you had not attacked or offended me first. Regardless of your claimed intention, I do not like it when you are doing something that displeases me.

No, it cannot help me since I see no benefit in your attack. *I* know what you *really* intend to do. (claiming to interpret the person's intentions better than they can.)

You are triggering something hidden deep in my mind that I am trying to suppress from the past. I have been successful in suppressing it and here you come along to bring it forth, out into the open. I am afraid of what you will expose. It may be small but I am sure it is devastating.

No, I do not remember what it was. It has been hidden for so long. You are bringing it out into the open where others can see it. I must attack you with words of anger to beat this frightening monster back down into the dungeons of my mind. This goes for anyone who dares to enter my dungeon to retrieve anything.

How dare you find the keys to my anxious subconscious doors (push my buttons)! Therein are my secrets! How dare you come so close to them! Even I do not remember what they are. Now I am terrified to see what is hidden there. It is possible I will not be able to emotionally handle what I discover. Surely, it can only cause me great emotional harm. My heart cannot endure more pain.

Anxiously I must fight to keep my past suppressed. Surely I suppress its secrets for my own protection. Since you seem to have found the keys, I fear you will attempt to once again unlock the doors of my painful secrets only to insist that I be punished again for them. For this reason, we will have conflict whenever we meet to assure you do not go poking around in my head again!

So what if I appear cold! My heart must be protected against you. I will not allow you to hurt me. It has happened to me before and I am sure you are the same as the others. You are all alike! I want to be loved by you, but now I cannot trust you since you have pried. Can you not just love me and not intrude in my fears?

It is dark there in my dungeon but you insist on bringing a light to make things visible. Take your light away this instant! It is causing me pain. Since it is pain you offer me, my attack against you is justified and deserving. How could I possibly welcome you into my heart let alone be loving? I cannot for fear you will bring that darn light again!

Besides, you are the one with the problem. What is in my dungeon has nothing to do with our conflict. I can clearly see who you are and do not want to mirror you. By finding fault in you, I can influence you to then become focused on your own issues and be out of my dungeon (affairs). Otherwise, I fear I cannot lock my doors again without your suspicious intrusion.

Why must I face my darkness? Deal with your own darkness because *you* certainly need to! Besides, I am just fine and doing better than you. Our conflict is fueled from your darkness. If you would just clear up your own stuff, mine will go away. Please try to see that! *You* are the cause of my problems, pain and stagnation. I cannot be. *You* are keeping away **my** joy!

Yet, I know I cannot be happy with or without you unless I confront my own darkness. Although my fear is strong, I am determined not to surrender to that light! My life could change drastically. That terrifies me because I do not know what that could mean. What if I cannot handle it?

End of dialogue

Our interpretations are based upon fear of the unknown and all of the what-ifs, so we respond from fear in the form of anger. Although what-ifs rarely happen, fear of them is great. As long as the ego can maintain fear in us, we will not discover that when we allow light to illuminate our darkness, there will only be an empty room ready for good to fill it up.

What-if situations are only in our minds. They are not real in the present but have been placed significantly in our anticipated future. Yet, neither place do they exist since the past nor the future exists today. The past is forever gone and the future has not yet come.

Anger is fear in a different form and a way to express guilt. Anger is an attempt to project the guilt that lies suppressed in our dungeon's darkness. We created the darkness to hide the guilt. Guilt is not necessarily warranted but we have taken possession of it. There are layers of guilt, which have hidden the original one. Those layers of guilt are many and have distorted the original guilt, presenting it in different forms to punish us. Guilt says we must be punished; therefore, we seek punishment, select one, and then call it bad luck. Now the ego has something new to distract us from our innocence.

The original guilt is the belief in our separation from God and thus we no longer have access to His Love. Therefore, we seek this Love through human beings or material things and call it love. When these sources cannot give us true Love or mock it to our needs, we become angry and the guilt is compounded. It is their fault we cannot find Love. If only they would cooperate. "You know what I need, so give it to me!" we insist.

One of the disguises of guilt in which anger hides is self-esteem. Self-esteem is affected by how we imagine others see us. When the image we have created for ourselves seems threatened, we become furious! Anger will then defensively appear in business, personal, and social relationships.

The situation is about to expose who we think we are, not who we are trying to portray. Neither of these forms of us is us, the facade nor the ego created self. Nevertheless, we will attack to protect them.

Guilt is also exposed when a loved one seems to be in danger. If something were to happen to them, it would add to the pile of guilt in the mind's dungeon or be a reminder of one that may already be there. Those things stored in that dungeon will be used by God to crucify us, we think. Yet, we are the ones who have been crucifying ourselves all of these years. We have refused to admit what we have done to ourselves. Acknowledgment would only add more guilt, the ego hopes.

Since this is merely an error in thinking created by the ego, it can be corrected. We are not dependent upon the ego for our thoughts; the ego is dependent upon us. Evict it at will. Evict all anger and the need to attack and thus take responsibility for all errors. After all, they are *our* errors. Making errors are not a life's sentence of any kind. Fortunately, all errors are correctable.

Let the light reveal the nothingness of the errors. Choose to release them. Release them to the Holy Spirit who has never forgotten how to correct them. Thus, they are no longer ours and we are free.

Chapter 15 - Exercise:

Take deep breaths often when doing the following exercise steps. Write down:

1. For three days, watch someone in the midst of expressing anger, regardless of the significance. It can be the same person or a different person each day.

    a. What is the topic? Observe the angry person's body, the environment, and the results.

    b. Watch the observers during the explosion.

    c. Note how the observers (sometimes the victim) returns to "life as usual" after all is said and done versus the one who does not.

2. Observe your own anger the rest of the week with the same eyes as in step 1 above.

    a. Are you angry for fear or loss of some kind: affection, self-image, what if, job, etc.?

    b. Are you angry because you are "supposed to be?"

    c. Is it triggering something of the past? (*Here we go again* episode?)

    d. Does it feel like a repeat offense?

3. In each case, what was the value of expressing the anger?

    a. Do you truly feel completely satisfied inside with your response? Is there more you would like to say or do?

    b. Why or why not?

4. As often as possible, let go of the conflict for as long as you can if only for an instant. Any time period counts. Repeat this step until it feels neutral. Take as many days, months, or years you need but commit to its release.

Note: It gets easier after the first release is accomplished to any degree. Try not to apply more than three at a time to this exercise on Resentment and Forgiveness.

16

Getting Beyond Disappointments

"Man is ever in search of strength. It is the strong man that wins. It is the man with power that scales the heights. To be strong is to be great; and it is the privilege of greatness to satisfy every desire, every aspiration, every need. But strength is not for the few alone; it is for all, and the way to strength is simple. Proceed this very moment to the mountaintops of the strength you now possess, and whatever may happen do not come down. Do not weaken under adversity." — Christian Larson

Christian Larson says, *"Resolve to remain as strong as determined and as highly enthused during the darkest night of adversity as you are during the sunniest day of prosperity. Do not feel disappointed when things seem disappointing. Keep the eye single upon the same brilliant future regardless of circumstances, conditions or events. Do not lose heart when things go wrong. Continue undisturbed in your original resolve to make all things go right. To be overcome by adversity and threatening failure is to lose strength. The man who never weakens when things are against him will grow stronger and stronger until all things will delight to be for him. He will finally have all the strength he may desire or need. Be always strong and you will always be stronger.*"[3]

Perhaps we have come to believe things always go wrong in our lives and seldom go right. If it were so, we would not have survived life so many years nor accomplished what we have today.

Many times such judgment is based upon comparison, which is categorized and accepted as good or bad in our experiences. Each experience has been defined by some external influence and accepted internally as true.

This definition is constantly reviewed in our minds, causing attraction to the very conditions not wanted in our current experiences. Changing the experience requires a mental request the mind must provide for the body to attract only good.

When the physical experience does not manifest as envisioned, the mind will simply interpret the experience as negative regardless of Truth. Truth is denied to satisfy the subconscious request to make the negative interpretation seem real. Although our perception may change, the Truth remains unchanged. Truth cannot be changed under any circumstances; however, it can be denied.

Truth is reality that does not change. Reality is God's creation and we have no power to change it, nor do we have the desire to change it. We have trained our eyes to see illusion rather than reality. What chaos and hopelessness there would be if the ego were allowed to change reality! Regardless of the chaos these ego thoughts may seem to create, our Spirit remains at peace for it never forgets Truth.

Kenneth Wapnick said, *"The guilt and fear induced by our beliefs in the ego's reality is the cause of all our suffering. It is the ego thoughts in our minds that paint unrest over the eternal calm of our minds as God created it. Letting go of that thought, even for an instant, brings immediate peace."*

We have chosen that our awareness be focused upon the external to create our world. The external, is aimless, destructive, and contradicts. Hence, many times our peace will seem clouded over in this stormy life.

When the storm frightens us, the ego may offer defiance as rescue from this nightmare. In this act of defiance, we become determined to fix things on our own. Life is out of control but with our own two hands, we will get it back in shape we claim. From this defiant conquest, we measure our strength, unaware we are really measuring our weakness.

This is not an act of maturity, intellect, or something to marvel, nor is it an act of strength as the ego has led us to believe; it is fuel on fire that weakens us even further. Chaos can only produce more chaos. It does not know how to produce anything else.

Having chosen chaos, ask, "What is the cost?" and "What is it I really fear?"

Answers to these questions will calculate the cost of holding onto fear. It will reveal the exchange of strength for weakness. Weakness is depleted

119

because strength is unlimited yet we give up or surrender to despair. Although the limitation of weakness is exposed, we still deny it. We obsessively seek material pacifiers that will ease our seeming hopelessness only to further prove there is weakness in addiction.

Our body and mind lay exhausted in a pool of tears. We feel we cannot win. Cannot win? But how could our little will be stronger than God's? Strength was not depleted by the limitations we placed upon our mind and body. Inner divine strength is neither measurable nor reducible. It is never weak.

Take this strength to a higher consciousness, bring it down to earth, and apply it to all activities and thoughts. All we need is within us. Therein awaits our army of strength and our carpenters of life. As we exercise this consciousness, all we need to do is put it into motion for our healing. The only thing stopping us is us. Only we can hold ourselves back.

We have trudged through the worse times thinking we could go no further, but we did. An inner strength emerged where true strength is stored in surplus. We reached deep with a determination to survive the journey at hand. All thought, action, and consciousness were focused on the goal.

Strengthened focus will lift us above the limitations of our mind and body. Negative action is conquered by this strength and forced to retreat. Negativity cannot win because we are never alone in our journey.

We can never be alone in any situation. God cannot be without Itself. Allowing our deep true strength to come through us may also mean changing what we define as strength and weakness. We may find it difficult to listen to something we feel is weak, to someone we feel is weak, to an opinion we feel is weak or to something we feel may weaken a belief. But we cannot be weakened. We can only deny our true strength.

Denial is all we can do to it. We were created as an extension of God. We cannot be weak. Strength is our natural inheritance. We may find ourselves in situations where we feel *helpless*. This is only an ego thought where it claims we are not in **control** of the situation. Control is an ego requirement.

To think we are in control implies that we do not need God's support, that we are helpless or hopeless. Yet, we have all the support and strength we need at any moment. When we feel we do not (and it is only a feeling), then reach out and use the strength of others. Be absolutely free to do that. Ignore the urgings of the ego that we are anything but smart in accessing Strength through others.

If we allow, the ego will shackle our mind, and for that instant, it will seem we cannot think. Well, we do not have to think. We can allow our Spirit to do it for us. It will communicate to God what we need done at that moment. Right before us, we allow strength to unfold in, through, and around us. Victory steps forth!

Chapter 16 - Exercise:

Write down:

Identify in your life who is special. Under what circumstances does he/she disappoint you?

1. Select a special friend or person.

2. Allow your special person to error without disappointment for the next 3 months.

3. Give others the same specialness you have defined for yourself whatever that might be. Experience the specialness you give.

4. Parents or mentors: Choose a child you have made special.

    a. Is the child disappointing whenever he/she does not fulfill or is weak at the specialness you have defined?

    b. Is that specialness role defined around your alleged personal childhood failure or shortcoming of some kind?

    c. Is the child to be what you could not, to prove a point or is it to fulfill the *child's* own dream?

17

Monster in the Closet

"For fear lies not in reality, but in the minds of children who do not understand reality. It is only their lack of understanding that frightens them, and when they learn to perceive truly they are not afraid."
— A Course In Miracles

Why can't God see my pain? Why does He let bad things happen? We ask these questions time and time again. We believe what we see, what we think we see, and what we imagine we see. The latter can be the most impressionable and deadly.

For example, when we watch a horror movie, it is our imagination that makes the movie most frightening. If there is a love scene, our imagination raises the passion in it. Our imagination is influenced by our own experiences or fantasies. A great deal of the movie is left to the viewer's imagination, which is what the producer desires to affect.

As adults, some of the things in the movie can be dismissed as amusing rather than horrible. We know it is not real. Knowledge takes us beyond the visual, which allows us to be entertained and appreciative of the creative skills used in making the movie.

On the other hand, children may take the movie monsters home with them, embodying what they perceived according to their own little imaginations, which may result in nightmares and paranoia. What was viewed in the movie portrayed the horribly mean things a monster can and will do to a human being as far as a child is concerned. Monsters are traditionally portrayed as ugly ferocious beasts lurking in the dark, ready to attack once its helpless victim is alone.

"Children perceive frightening ghosts, monsters and dragons, and they are terrified. Yet if they ask someone they trust for the meaning of what they perceive, and are willing to let their own interpretations go in favor of reality, their fear goes with them. When a child is helped to translate his 'ghost' into a curtain, his 'monster' into a shadow, and his 'dragon' into a dream he is no longer

afraid, and laughs happily at his own fear." [4]

"You, my child, are afraid of your brothers and of your Father and of yourself. But you are merely deceived in them. Ask what they are of the Teacher of Reality, and hearing His answer, you too will laugh at your fears and replace them with peace. For fear lies not in reality, but in the minds of children who do not understand reality. Only their lack of understanding frightens them, and when they learn to perceive truly they are not afraid. And because of this they will ask for truth again when they are frightened." [5]

When you were a child, frightened of the monster lurking in your dark closet, it was real for you. This monster was fierce in the dark with its long fangs, iron jaws, and huge claws!

It is bedtime, which means lights out and time to sleep. After watching that horror movie, you are in no way sleepy and your eyes are wide open as you strain to pan the dark bedroom for that monster. As you do, you notice the closet door is ajar although you are certain it was closed before the light was turned off.

The monster must be watching, waiting for your parents to fall asleep before attacking you. You are sure you saw its enormous shadow cast upon the wall as your eyes darted toward the door. This was enough proof it existed. It was not pretend. The monster **was** real! It was no longer at the theater or in the television, but had followed you home somehow and snuck into your bedroom closet! Nothing could convince you otherwise. Nothing!

Your mind races in terror with thoughts of the awful things the monster will do to you. Too afraid to move, you tearfully scream out, "Mommeeeee!" What if mommy does not make it there in time when you cry out? Surely, the monster will devour you whole.

However, mommy always made it there before the monster attacked, to calm you and dry your tears. Even though the monster was still in the closet, you felt safe with mommy or daddy nearby. It could not get you now.

As mommy or daddy, you rushed to comfort your frightened child. You wanted so much for your child to feel secure and loved. You neither saw the monster nor were you interested in seeing it. What mattered most was to take away your child's fear. Proof the monster existed was not required for you to love and comfort your child. Comfort was given willingly without seeing what was only in the child's mind.

Regardless of how real the monster seemed to the child, any proof it existed or how often it came back, did not waver your knowing that this monster did not exist, now or ever. It was merely a character created only to entertain viewers from the big screen at the movie theatre.

Upon entering the child's room, you used light to help take away the fear. Instantly the fear was drastically reduced. The light revealed what was really creating the shadow on the wall. With this knowledge, life was good again and safe.

Now, the monster *did* cause some unwanted behavior at times such as disrupting a pleasant night's sleep. Monsters can be very real to a child. Upon each cry out for help, you lovingly responded to comfort who was an extension of you, your child. Sometimes your response took longer than other times because you knew there was no danger. However, it was important to respond since the child could become a danger to him/herself.

Children grow in their own time. With time, you knew the illusion would go away and the child would grow to see that there was never a monster.

You did not make the monster happen just as God does not make your illusions happen. Something impressive created or reinforced some illusions for you. Though they seem very real, you too will grow to see the illusions for what they are, nothing.

Chapter 17 - Exercise:

1. Recall a nightmare from your childhood or a recent one.

2. What were your thoughts when you awakened from the dream?

3. Recall a noise you heard. Was it the wind, a branch tapping against the house, a pet, etc.?

4. How fast did your fear disappear once the noise was identified?

5. If you did not clarify the source of the noise, what was the inner chatter?

18

You Are Special

"Everything good comes from the Presence of God within you. You must give this Presence your attention and your allegiance. God put something inside of us that will not let us down." — His Presence

Famous people are placed in a role of specialness when they are alive and even long after they are dead. At times, we expect from them everlasting youth, the best of life's joys, immunity to harm, and immortality. If certain things happen to them, then it is tragic. If certain things do not happen to them as we had stereotyped it should, then it is unfair. Blame is turned toward God, "Why does He let bad things happen to good people?"

Special groups and individuals can be made up of those we love, admire, pity, or hate such as:

| Our Children | Rich People | Single Mothers | Elderly |
| Hitler | Minorities | Boss | Foreigners |

Princess Diana	Handicapped	Lawyers	Homeless
Gay	Intellectuals	Doctors	Ghandi

The specialness given to each of us is often used to define self-worth, dispel guilt, or prove the ego's judgments about us are real. If *unfair* things happen to the good ones and good things happen to the *bad* ones, we say that, God must be weak to "allow" it. He seems to have no power over these things; therefore, something must be done about it. So we begin a campaign against what God has *allowed* to happen. It is a useless ego attack on God, to believe God has no power over these things.

These things are choices each individual made; things they created for their human experience. Life's experiences are choices God has granted. Each one was given the gift of choice, as to how their Spiritual Being would live as a human being. Spiritual Beings are ageless and choose whether to have a human experience lasting only as a child or beyond retirement.

The special person and us become victims of all alleged unfairness of the world. For those who allow, the Holy Spirit can redirect our seeming victimhood to have positive and meaningful impact on each other's lives.

Victimization creates exclusion, where the ego draws additional strength. Relationships become fragmented, which fuels chaos. Chaos usually results from judgments where comparison is inevitable. One special group becomes opposed to another, because ones specialness is defined as more worthy of forgiveness than another.

Specialness does not share. Sometimes it may have the appearance of joining for a *cause*, but is used only to strengthen or justify a claim to victimization relative to the other's cause. When genuine interest in another's alleged victimization is no longer the draw, force against Truth becomes the cause.

The ego recruits more proof of its reality and power and does not unite victims. For example, the elderly and the single mother may unite for more government funds and health programs supportive of their well-being. In another light, the elderly person may condemn the single mother and judge her harshly; the single mother may scorn the elder's race or culture.

This feeds still another specialness (moral values, racism, etc.) used as justification to encourage further separation of special people or groups, which nurtures the ego's existence.

Our unfair treatment seems real. Resultant pain makes it extremely difficult to ignore and to be unbelievable. To ignore the pain feels like denial of reality and betrayal of its victims. This presents confusion, fear, and a hint of guilt.

Our minds think, "What if it is real and we do not do something about it? We could go to hell, suffer (get what is coming to us), or as punishment, lose something we value. We must do something about it. We must save the special people." In desperate fear, we make ourselves *special* because of our commitment to *helping* the special people, and then label it as being a *concerned citizen*.

Fear has driven us to fix what God does not seem to be able to control; therefore, we take control in the name of God to *help* Him fix things. It feels good because now the world sees us, acknowledges us, and periodically reports on our wonderful contributions to humanity.

Certainly, God will look more loving upon us for caring for His special people, for helping Him to complete what He could not. From this, we have established our worth within our own mind. We are loved, have no guilt, and have sacrificed and earned our worthiness. Now it is okay to have our desires.

Fear goes underground as if to disappear forever. However, when all we worked for begins to pay off, fear resurfaces. Fear of loss becomes strong again, except now it is fear of loss of material gain and our special rank of worthiness (self-worth). On this, we have built our new self-esteem.

What we have read about ourselves and heard about ourselves is now who we think we are. Fear becomes anger, fully justified, invested to secure who we think we are. The ego now offers us a new victimhood. We are special, the media and public have said so; our specialness must be protected.

This is the trap that starts with *good intentions* then ends up corrupt. It happens so often with good people. They are still good people with good intentions, except now controlled by fear. *"What you have given specialness has left you bankrupt and your treasure house barren and empty, with an open door inviting everything that would disturb your peace to enter and destroy.*" [6]

Since the Holy Spirit treats no one special, He can override the ego's intent and create a holy situation with our relinquishment of the fear surrounding it. *"You can place any relationship under His care and be sure that it will not result in pain, if you offer Him your willingness to have it serve no need but His."* [7] We must surrender our own agendas completely.

Chapter 18 - Exercise:

Identify in your life who is special. Under what circumstances?

1. Who is your idol or mentor?
2. Why did you choose him/her?
3. What do you think they have that you do not?

19

You Are Forgiven

*"The fire of faith burns away all doubt and
sees only possibilities. Through prayer, we
awaken from the imaginary, move into the
real, and feel at home in the universe."*
— Dr. Michael Beckwith

Atonement was sent for everyone, no
exceptions. Jesus accepted the Atonement
for us. The Atonement is a conscious
acknowledgment of the truth and acceptance that
the past is no longer effective or valid in our lives.
When the Atonement is accepted, healing, peace,
and joy accompany it, just as wet accompanies
water.

The Atonement grants freedom from all past
errors. Those errors cannot exist in the present, only
in the past. Since the past no longer exists, only the
mind can conjure up something non-existent then
respond to it as real. Mental resurrection of the past
does not deem it real whatsoever.

In emotional defense of a current situation, the mind will retrieve the past, respond as if the past was real today, and then declare it is being held hostage by the past. Only the mind's imagination is holding the mind hostage because the past and present cannot exist simultaneously. We can only emotionally relive the whole drama of the past since we cannot truly recreate the past. Reliving it is a desperate attempt to change it because the Atonement has been overlooked or not believed to be applicable in this case.

Eventually it becomes difficult to overlook what we have attempted to make real. What we have made real is merely pretense since we cannot create true reality. Reality existed before our inception; we cannot alter it. What seems unalterable feels like the error was not corrected. As a result, guilt is evoked and a place to project it is sought. That place is often another person who is close to us.

Claiming and creating any guilt, imposed or seemingly appropriate for an error, requires the creation of a special relationship. Guilt insists upon conflict. The special relationship in which conflict develops chaos, adverse situations, and violent situations is where atonement becomes necessary. Somehow, guilt has elements held valuable which justify the type of relationship it will be and how we will communicate in that relationship.

Guilt communicates with conflict and a victim is created. Victimization becomes valuable and serves other purposes in the relationship such as tangible excuses and explanations of our misery. Perceived victimization in the relationship becomes a way in which we seek to relinquish responsibility for our miserable world.

The ego will encourage suppression of love toward the special person, treat them unlovingly or ban them from parts or all of our lives. Whatever the case, it is strongly ego-driven and thus functionless in our journey and spiritual growth. It blinds us of the Atonement that has already happened and depletes our fragile self-esteem.

Insatiable vengeance feeds our starving self-esteem with empty substance. Vengeance merely preserves the past to abuse our mind, often weakening it to a state of deep depression. Such self-abuse need not be. It is unwarranted self-hatred.

There is nothing we have done to deserve it. We should not let the ego convince us otherwise.

In time, we will tire of this hatred for it strengthens our belief in a separation from God's Love. Losing God's love would be devastating. Although it is impossible to be without this Love, it is possible to totally deny it in any form such that we no longer recognize it or feel worthy of it. Remember, we are always worthy of Love. As we accept this Love, the Atonement becomes more recognizable in our lives as our innocence is restored.

Welcome the Atonement into the day's affairs. Welcome it by offering any valued past to the Holy Spirit who will restore all innocence. Hold nothing back. Offer all errors in faith, without judgment, and regardless of the past. Completely empty this storehouse of guilt and loveless thoughts. Take full advantage of this opportunity of inner peace. All that we bring forth is forgiven in an instant and made peaceful. No exceptions.

At first, it may be difficult to let go of these things, leaving them in the hands of the Holy Spirit, when we do not believe how much God truly loves us. God's love is 100% unconditional. His Love is unlimited and of no cost. Nothing on earth can compare with this pure Love. All that we want forgiven, is. And we can let go of the nightmares of the threatening hell. Heaven is our destination.

Chapter 19 – Exercise:

1. Write down an incident of the past that brings about feelings of guilt every time you just think about it.

2. Who defined the guilt?

3. How real is it?

4. Who is involved in the incident?

5. Do you want to release yourself from the incident?

6. Write down why you need to keep this guilt.

7. Write down why not.

8. Write down the benefits of what you concluded from step 6.

9. Write down the benefits of what you concluded from step 7.

10. Since God has no interest in, nor does He condemn you of what is listed in step 1, it is time to let it go.

11. Once you are able to release it, even if just for a moment, write down what you feel. When the ego starts telling you that you are not progressing, remember that moments become minutes, become hours, become days, become months, and then become years. Let's get started.

20

Resentment and Forgiveness

"Hating people Is like burning down your own house to get rid of a rat."
— Harry Emerson Fosdick

Is there a sense of failure of some kind? Are you concerned about your image; what will people think? Do you feel betrayed or victimized? These things bring superficial value or justification to hold resentment in our hearts. Our egos will appear to support our guarded reasons for not relinquishing the resentment, yet it uses these reasons to force guilt and self-punishment upon ourselves.

Forgiveness is not a pardon or a weakening of who we are. It is a rejection of the ego's perception. It is not a denial of what took place, but we no longer have to live in its madness or under its control. There is power in forgiveness for it frees

144

our body, mind and life to move forward productively. It allows us to go beyond error to where we experience Love. Only its experience can truly explain love's benefit and the peace it brings.

Choose peace instead of resentment. Release the resentment fully without judgment or expectation. Visualize nothing of how the response should be or what it should look like for emotional freedom is the goal.

Sometimes we allow the happiest moment to be shattered by the ego. Whenever we seem to be having too much fun or are too happy, the ego draws from the past and whispers, "You are not worthy of it, after all you have done!" or "It won't last!" Subsequently we sabotage our joy by sentencing ourselves to more self-punishment, and then blame God or others for the pain. We become their victim.

Through resentment, we have made ourselves victims. Resentment is based upon issues of the past where we continue to dwell as if we really still live there. The past is gone forever. It can never be given back. Thus, past issues return only in our minds. These issues exist no more in reality but are often re-created subtly through different experiences we are now having.

Often we have heard ourselves say, "I keep doing the same thing; the story of my life; I keep choosing the same type of man/woman; I knew I shouldn't have done that again."

Other times we find ourselves not able to resist making a choice we **knew** would later give us grief. The seeming forbidden was irresistible. These are all chaotic habits offered by the ego to keep us on a fictitious joyous path, where joy can never be reached.

Perhaps even the same emotions from a past issue show up again in a present *like* experience. This is yet a past experience re-enacted as if it were real in the present. In reality, it is not happening again. Still we find ourselves unable to *let go* because the pain seems so real and so present.

There is something in this pain the ego has convinced us is valuable, there is something to gain, it urges. However, the gain is not really toward the present issue at all. The past is still interfering and fuming the battle. The battle has little chance of ending since the opponents are not both addressing the pain they think is between them.

To satisfy the ego, revenge brings a past pain to the present. Revenge for a past issue is acted out in present situations where we cannot possibly gain satisfaction since we cannot truly go back to the past let alone change it. It is insatiable and no longer a part of this current human experience regardless of our emotional experiences or manifestations of our ego thoughts. This insatiable pain festers guilt.

Guilt becomes a corpse we try to discard through others via blame. Although defined by the ego, guilt is often accepted as valid. One of the things the body is used for is guilt. Guilt searches opportunities of punishment and finds it wherever it can, especially through resentment. Guilt-ridden thoughts reinforce the fear of punishment, keeping forgiveness well hidden.

Until one accepts forgiveness, the body will be a target for more self-punishment. Guilt conceals itself in the body. It picks a part of the body and with hatred, builds its home, taking the form of disease, stress or addiction of some type. Sometimes the intrusion is so violent it appears life threatening. As the intrusion becomes more intense, the ego's offer of death becomes an appealing escape for the body. At that moment, such an escape seems to be the only way to peace.

Just as easily as the ego gave us this guilt, we can give it back to its unkind creator, since it is a lie belonging only to the ego. Now is the time to return this borrowed illusion. We have no need of it.

How to let go of guilt or let go of being a victim? Ask for forgiveness of the resentment then ask to be able to accept that forgiveness. When we can accept that we have indeed been forgiven, self-forgiveness takes place. Self-forgiveness can be the most difficult part of letting go of resentment.

How often have we apologized, heard it accepted, yet doubted its sincerity? Judgment of someone's body language, tone of voice, the attitude, or worthiness were all used to weaken our ability to accept the forgiveness offered to us.

These factors then influenced subsequent attempts at amends intended to convince us of sincere forgiveness. For some reason, forgiveness remained unbelievable, and instead, we accepted its shackles.

There is freedom in forgiveness and self-forgiveness. Not being able to allow the amendment to happen leaves us alone in that belief, creating a separation and thus loneliness. This loneliness imprisons our minds in the cells of resentment, victimization and guilt where joy cannot enter.

Sometimes obsessive attempts to make amends seem necessary. Resentment builds to enormous heights for not being able to *fix things* with the other person(s) to our satisfaction. Perhaps others do not respond to our attempts as we think they should. The response falls short of meeting our expectations. Consequently, the relationship is strained. Still, we must forgive.

Forgive and accept forgiveness. Let the issue go. There is no loss in accepting forgiveness and there is an opportunity to develop a healthy relationship. In the event there is reluctance to make the amend, step back and listen. Recognize the ego's words sprinting through one's mind. Try again to let go. Try until forgiveness can be held in the heart even for just an instant. The more we forgive, the more we will because it becomes familiar.

After we have forgiven and accepted forgiveness, we must give it to the Holy Spirit who knows what to do with it. That is Its function. Do nothing more. Rest and give it no more attention. Feel the burden lifted. We can experience the peace always present in spite of what appears to be happening around us. The peace within us will remain unshaken.

While our human self may be emotionally shattered, the true Self remains at peace. Through this peace, the ego is hushed. Its thunderous criticism is muted for it cannot overpower the Voice within us. The ego cannot intrude anymore; it can only be invited. Our human emotions are healed and calmed as we allow the gentle Voice to guide us in re-molding the chaos of our human lives into one of peace.

Be still and let it.

Chapter 20 - Exercise:

Write down:

1. Identify two resentments in your life, the oldest resentment you have and the newest one.

2. What are the similarities between the two?

3. Name four people you resent.

4. Write down the buttons they push(ed).

5. In what other ways are these people able to control your life?

6. Do they ruin your day when you see them?

7. Do they take away a level of joy when you see them or take it away entirely?

8. Can they create tension in your house even without their presence?

9. How often do you avoid places where they may be present?

10. Do you avoid being with friends he/she has?

11. Do you avoid social events where they may be in attendance?

12. Write down an incident of the past that feels real every time you just think about it.

13. How real is it?

14. Who is involved in the incident?

15. Each day, emotionally release yourself from the incident even if just for a moment. Try this every day until you achieve it.

16. Once you are able to release it, even if just for a moment, write down what you feel.

21

Think For Yourself

"My whole, divine filled life is an adventure in self-discovery. With confidence, I make the decision to step out into the unknown where new gifts and talents emerge from my divine connection with God."

— Helen Gordon

Who is making the decisions about our lives? All decisions we make are based upon events, results and experiences of the past. They are influenced by belief systems we have accepted to either direct our lives or protect them. These belief systems were built from learned behavior, cultural influences, religious or spiritual practices, social consequences and fear, casting aside sane choices. The results of these decisions weigh heavily upon our self-esteem. Sometimes the results build our confidence with success or brings great embarrassment.

Approval:

Learned Behavior.

You chose Uncle Bob as your role model. You wanted to be *just like him.* He was successful by your definition and observation. Everyone was proud of him, looked up to him and marveled at his success. As a result, you observed and selectively copied his behavior because he had all the material desires that represent success. It seemed to have worked for him. He may have even noticed your ambition and helped you develop this behavior he had seemingly perfected.

Eventually time depleted your memory of who you were before this learned behavior. In your mind, you successfully destroyed the person you thought you did not want to be. Now you believe the new and improved person is who you are. Anything that threatens to restore your memory of who you really are is considered hostile; therefore, you attack it out of fear of losing who you have become.

Who you are was not allowed to develop and is a complete stranger to you now, a fearful unknown. What you can become terrifies you. You have no idea what you might become; therefore, you reject the development of this stranger. It is very uncomfortable. To take a risk of being yourself is just too frightening because it is a stranger to you. This stranger is a threat to your current reality and comfort zone whether your current life is comfortable or not.

Rejection:
Cultural Influence.

Some of the behaviors you embodied may have been altered so as not to conflict with your culture. Cultures have beginnings from ancient pasts and are honored without question. Behavior in conflict with your culture we think may threaten separation of some kind. You do not desire to be an outcast or rejected from your family, friends or culture for fear of being alone, loveless or disappointing. To hurt or disappoint them would invite guilt and possible shame.

Rejection is experienced as separation. It is an exclusion of sorts that creates fear. Whom could you turn to in time of despair? Whom could you talk to that would understand first hand what you are going through? Someone not of your culture might not understand and ridicule you.

To leave a life you know in order to learn a new one is terrifying. Life would be too difficult you think. You have no idea what to expect or what is expected of you. "Would you ever be accepted?" races through your mind. A new life is just too uncomfortable, fearful and uncertain.

Exclusion:
Religious or Spiritual Practices.

The meaning of salvation has been taught to you in many different forms. The only meaningful goal becomes salvation. Traditionally, it is taught that if you cannot reach this goal then you have sinned or have failed in your belief and have failed God. Either one feels like a betrayal of God so you feel guilty and doomed to eternal punishment of some kind.

This belief must be addressed in your decision so that you avoid guilt. In an attempt to convince you that you have reason to feel guilty, the ego will stuff your bed of life with guilt where your dreams become nightmares.

You see yourself on the excluded list, among the unwanted, a fugitive of your own misery. The ego tells you that God does not want you and has set you aside among the unwanted, and separated Himself from you. Again, a sense of separation is being shoved into your thoughts; these thoughts falsely verify your unworthiness and remind you of past failures of all kinds, big and small.

Relationships go sour. Others at work are promoted when you are the most qualified. Backstabbing and betrayal become constant occurrences in many areas of your life. Health issues come and go affecting your ability to control your life.

What has happened is that you are attracting to you your belief of unworthiness. Since you think you are unworthy and unwanted of God, the ego declares you must be punished and sentenced to suffering.

Acceptance:

Social Consequences.

Social definitions say that if you meet certain physical, emotional or intellectual requirements, you will be liked. Perhaps you become obsessed by just one of these social requirements to compensate for an area in which you feel lacking or feel it impossible for you to meet these constraints. You fear if you are not liked then you will not be accepted. Rejection is an awful feeling. Without acceptance, it seems impossible to be successful.

This fear drives you to attempt the impossible. The urgent goal now is to satisfy all constraints you have imposed upon yourself. Those in which you may fall short are hidden through manipulation or covered up in some manner. Guilt then drives you. Neither contentment nor peace result from making a decision from a place of guilt based upon things already decided. That is, once you have deemed the thing as negative, and then deny it exists, the guilt is simply projected elsewhere. It leads to exhaustive manipulation to suppress the thing even further.

Manipulation usually requires you break one of your own rules and thus you have failed even yourself. When you fail, you become fearful. From this, you begin to make more fear-based decisions. Decisions are based upon your recent past from rules inherited from your ancestors' past. Each decision was based upon external influences. They were not yours. Your partner in the decision was the ego.

Therefore, your decisions create conflict between satisfying your ego-driven rules and satisfying your Mind. The ego is forever applying a different interpretation according to the immediate gratification. Rules easily change accordingly. Many years have been invested in creating your way of life. It will not be easy to let it go.

Life feels predictable for you and comfortable. It has become very valuable as it is. Eventually, sacrifice, loss, sense of failure, guilt and fear battle in your mind manifesting as a headache or other stress related illness.

Through these negative elements, the ego confirms your unworthiness. If you had just not failed, you would be worthy. If you could just keep this failure hidden, no one would know of your unworthiness. They would accept you (who they think you are). How wonderful life would be if the failure could be transformed into success, then you could be worthy again. Once again, you could be wanted, adored and have love returned. Joy could be restored.

The affects of one "wrong-decision" (ego-based decision) have a domino affect on subsequent decisions. The madness begins where peace is blocked and obscured beyond recognition.

Think for Yourself

Awareness of the decisions you make will set you free. Clarity will light your path. Not only your own, but decisions of others will be better understood. What they are not saying becomes louder than what they are saying aloud. From this understanding, you will gain compassion for others, self-love and the end of chaos. Life will respond to you in the most magnificent way.

Chapter 21 - Exercise:

Write down:

1. Who influences the major decisions in your life?

2. If it is not you, have you been happy with their choices for you?

3. Why or why not?

4. Look at a decision you made 5 years ago. Were you pleased with the outcome?

5. If not, how would you change the decision?

6. If you did, how would you change the decision? (this is not a typo)

22

Your Body, A Sacrifice

*"The body converts emotional pain into the
form of a stress-related disease."*
— Helen Gordon

Pain, the lack of pleasure, becomes depression when it is internalized. When this internalization of pain depletes the body of mental alertness and physical energy, the resultant feeling becomes judged as *tired*. More sleep is required. Sleeping then becomes an escape from the pain's source. Increased periods of sleep intensify the attachment to the pain. This is where suffering begins resulting in mental and physical deterioration.

The body converts emotional pain into the form of a stress-related disease such as high blood pressure, heart malfunctions, over-weight, under-weight, hair loss, chronic illness, worsened allergies, and more.

The pain being referenced here is mental pain seeking expression through the body as an attempt to be heard. It is imperative this pain is released for it manifests itself in many destructive expressions. For example, remembrance of an incidence that brought us pain becomes anger, which ultimately affects all areas of our lives.

The reluctance to invite a loving opportunity into our lives is influenced by the anticipation of more pain. Anxiety and fear raise their vicious heads to whisper discouraging words to us. Surely the pain will come again we are told. This certainty of pain becomes so strong that it paralyzes movement out of an unwanted situation. Subsequent decisions are influenced by this pre-determined future, which is based upon fear.

Lists of reasons, excuses, or illnesses are collected to prove our pain real. It supports and justifies our decisions. The list is intended to lessen our guilt about the outcome of our lives.

To shift the responsibility of our life's condition, people are selected to blame for our stagnation, failures, and incompetence. Usually those closest to us are chosen since they are frequently in our presence or in communication.

If these people and reasons were not there, life would be wonderful we claim. Surely the world will agree when we show them all our list of proof! Actually, we chose fear. We chose to hold on to the pain through constant pursuits of insatiable revenge, obsolete grudges, and whiny self-pity.

Pain can only stay where it is invited and as long as permitted. Holding on to the pain is self-destructive. Since self-destruction contradicts the fear of destruction, this choice is not what we truly desire anyway. It is love we truly desire.

The attention and superficial love received through illness is pacifying but not satisfying. It cheats us and the giver out of the exchange of real love. Careful the illness does not draw our giver into also choosing illness in some form. Some refer to this as sympathy pain.

The giver feels guilty that their life is going well in spite of our pain. The ego has convinced the giver that it would only be *fair* to experience pain as well. Sympathy pain also seems to lessen the giver's obligation to give more time or energy expected of the relationship.

Others' prolonged, chronic, or repetitive illness can invite resentment. Life was joyous doing pleasant things, now that time must be rationed with an unpleasant situation. Although the giver resents the illness, the response is experienced as a direct attack on the relationship.

Whether our pain is just starting or has been long term, self-forgiveness is necessary. Also, we must forgive anyone we have blamed for the pain. Pain can only be fully released through forgiveness.

Starting from the by-product of the pain, that which is visible, begin to peel away the layers of original causes of the pain. The pain may be great right now because it has been fed, strengthened, justified, validated and wrapped in layers of ego responses. Going directly to the core of it can distort it or be overwhelmingly terrifying. However, peeling layers one at a time reveals the paths this pain has taken in our lives. What really needs healing is then clarified. Now the problem can be treated affectively.

So do not hurry or worry about progress. Be patient. Like an onion, as we peel away layers of the pain, tears will come as we near the core. However, the tears subside as our wholeness is lovingly restored. Celebrate each layer. Each layer is progress toward lessening the pain until there is nothing more to peel.

Chapter 22 - Exercise:

This is an exercise toward becoming more aware of your body's responses to people, situations and things.

Become aware of your *eyebrows* this week when:

1. Chatting with someone you like vs. someone you don't like.

2. Driving long distance vs. short distance.

3. While watching television

4. Listening to music.

5. When a toddler smiles at you.

6. Change *eyebrows* to *breathing* and repeat steps 1-5.

7. Change *breathing* to *lips* and repeat steps 1-5.

23

Change Happens

"In change is the gift of peace, power and piety. What we become is larger than our expectations; what we gain is beyond our expectations; what we learn is beyond what we thought intellectually capable."
— Helen Gordon

Change is terrifying, awkward, and unpredictable. We fear that anticipated controversy created by the change could threaten the loss of our external valuables such as approval, loved ones, material things, livelihood, social status, and love.

Heaven forbid we change our image by which the world knows and respects us! What will people say? What will become of it? After all, we worked hard all our lives to get where we are now. We certainly do not want to lose it or start over.

The need for change is clear, leaving us anxious. The need to change haunts us. Peace of mind will escape us until we open to change. In change is the gift of peace, power and piety. What we become is larger than our expectations; what we gain is beyond our expectations; what we learn is beyond what we thought intellectually capable.

The ego says it would remove the masks we have created and expose our vulnerability. We may believe that if our vulnerability is exposed our persuasive power is lost in both personal and business relationships. Perhaps, one of the saddest things we do is define love by power. For many this is how they experience love.

We may have to give up self-pity, our way of receiving superficial love through negative attention. Too often, we sit on the pity-pot welcoming sympathy from whoever is willing to give it as if it were a priceless treasure!

Change may also mean that we will have to forgive. If we forgive someone for circumstances in our life, where can we place the blame for our failures and shortcomings as they occur?

Forgiveness means giving up judgments, stereotypes, fear and hate through which we seek victory of revenge. Instead, we have to give true love. Well isn't that ironic! Now we have to give what we have been seeking all the time through superficial means.

The opportunity for real love is ours, so cautiously we grab it. Mixed emotions of fear and joy set in because we do not know what to do with real love. It seems so foreign and of a different language or world.

Let doubt and fear be gone forever. Accept what goes with love to replenish it. Thunder, lightning, and rain are necessary for the reproduction of the beauty and life of the earth from which man was created. For what follows, is the warmth of the sunshine simply to magnify life's brilliance and earth's beauty!

Chapter 23 - Exercise:

Write down:

1. One thing where more than three people have hinted or suggested you change something (including your doctor or boss).

2. One thing you think you should change.

3. What are the benefits of changing it?

4. One thing you do not want to change ever.

5. The benefits of not making that change.

6. One thing you think you can easily change.

7. A date to start it and a date to achieve it.

24

Miracles Happen

"Miracles do not obey the laws of this world. They merely follow from the laws of God." — A Course In Miracles Lesson 77

Often we are in awe of miracles but miracles are a normal occurrence. Rather than *expecting* miracles to happen, we *hope* they happen. Some of us think that some angelic virtue, anointing or *specialness* will grant us worthiness of a miracle. Not until we satisfy one or all of these criteria do we expect a miracle.

Satisfying these criteria says we have qualified for a miracle and thus one can be granted. We have earned it. Many religions encourage a sacrifice or ritual of some kind as a means of qualification yet not guaranteeing a miracle. Sacrifices and rituals often attract failure and guilt to us.

The ego claims that there must have been something we did not do or did do to disqualify us of the miracle we requested. These requirements respond to the laws of the world. They do not change the laws of God in any way. In fact, the laws of God do not require sacrifices or rituals of any kind.

Some even quantify these worldly requirements as measurement for the application of the miracle. Traces of the disorder are expected to vary accordingly. If the disorder is financial, the miracle may be to have funds to pay a particular bill. Having met all criteria to the highest degree may provide funds beyond all bills and/or expenses creating excess and unimaginable wealth.

Often a petition to God for a financial blessing is conservative. We do not want to ask for too much we think. Paying one bill does not require less effort of God to pay all bills. Our egos throw the guilt of greed before us, as if we could possibly bankrupt God. Bankrupting God is a true impossibility! Dare give it a try!

Knowing this with all your mind and with all your heart is extremely powerful. Nothing can withstand its strength or certainty. Now rituals of the world *can* bring about positive results just as if the laws of God were actually being addressed. Understand though why some rituals *appear* to work for us.

An Example:

With a petition in mind, we set up an altar in an area designated as sacred space, light a candle, and then position ourselves comfortably before it. Recite a chant or silently meditate to enter a more relaxed state of consciousness. While doing this with closed eyes, concentrate on the flame of a candle. This lasts from minutes to hours. The ritual is repeated for some period of time, at a specified time of the day, to assure that the petition is answered as envisioned.

Perhaps we have experienced a ritual such as this in variations or witnessed such. What has happened is that it removes mental blocks of doubt for a moment. The solitude and focus eliminate all thoughts that might be distracting and attracts the desire. All judgments are laid aside for that moment.

For an instant, suspend all thought, which invites a state of mind in which to *expect* positive results. It provides that moment of suspension of all distractions and thoughts. We remain aware only of the spiritual connection being sought and become free to receive what we seek. This is no more than faith gradually strengthened. Faith opens the doors of miracles to us.

Note, a ritual may be something we need but it is **not** necessary. It takes us where we already are. Practice instant faith, rather than working yourself up to it. It is the inner Self that communicates during that moment of suspension, giving faith power, while the outer self applies it.

What we ask for in faith is certain. Our faith need not be perfect; it only need be in our minds for an instant. What is faith? Faith is letting God know that we are ready to accept the gift that has always been available to us.

Allow and trust the Holy Spirit to deliver it by means it knows that best responds to the petition. A miracle request fortunately is not judged or rated. All have an equal chance of a certain response.

There is no qualifying for miracles, as the ego would have us believe. There are no categories or size criteria in the mind of God. To think this would be placing limitations on the power of God. Fulfilling one request does not minimize the response to another and would imply competition for blessings that are equal and freely given.

Allow God to do what He loves to do, give us the Kingdom, that is, overflow our life with blessings waiting for us just for the asking. Regardless of the opinion of the ego, it **is** this simple. Eventually we will no longer need to perform any rituals or make any sacrifices to receive what is our right, a miracle! Just as Jesus, each of us is a child of God, whom He loves dearly. Jesus always refers to us as his brothers in the New Testament. He sees us on the same level.

Remember, only the ego sees levels, categories, and sizes. Although this may be difficult at first to accept, Jesus came here as an example, not an exception. He emphasizes this in the New Testament when He says, *"Anyone who has faith in me will do what I have been doing. He will do even greater things than these, because I am going to the Father."* [8] This implies that we have the same power and access to God as He did. He wanted to prove it by entering into a human form as we are. He shows us how by example.

We are powerful beings afraid of our power and our ego knows this. We have access to that power just as Jesus did. The Holy Spirit reminds us how God is a whole and we are extensions of God, a part of that whole. As Jesus says, we all make up the body of Christ. We are all a part of the one body.

"For we were all baptized by one Spirit into one body-whether Jews or Greeks, slave or free-and we were all given the one Spirit to drink.

Now the body is not made up of one part but of many. If the foot should say, 'Because I am not a hand, I do not belong to the body,' it would not for that reason cease to be part of the body.

But in fact, God has arranged the parts in the body, every one of them, just as he wanted them to be.

If they were all one part, where would the body be? As it is, there are many parts, but one body.

The eye cannot say to the hand, 'I don't need you!' And the head cannot say to the feet, 'I don't need you!'

On the contrary, those parts of the body that seem to be weaker are indispensable, and the parts that we think are less honorable we treat with special honor. And the parts that are unpresentable are treated with special modesty, while our presentable parts need no special treatment. But God has combined the members of the body and has given greater honor to the parts that lacked it, so that there should be no division in the body, but that its parts should have equal concern for each other.

If one part suffers, every part suffers with it; if one part is honored, every part rejoices with it.

Now you are the body of Christ, and each one of you is a part of it." [9]

This passage says that not one person is any more important than another is. Everyone is equally necessary and benefit from each other's blessings.

We often have rituals that take us to a more pure understanding, but abandon it once we think that we no longer need it. Because once we *know* things, we are more able to accept them. These (rituals) are training wheels of sorts. We need these things until we become more stable and confident.

Some things we find difficult to believe and accept just on word of mouth. We have to "see for ourselves." When that does happen, we must hold on to that faith and apply it at all times.

Chapter 24 - Exercise:

1. Has your perception of a miracle changed since reading this chapter?

2. Write down your definition of a miracle.

3. Write down the miracle(s) you want (with no limits).

4. If the inner critic is chattering, do you believe what it is saying? If so, why?

5. What is this inner critic trying to do?

6. Are you going to let it?

Footnotes

1. <u>A Course In Miracles</u>. (Tiburon, CA: Foundation for Inner Peace, 1985) 1.

2. Ibid, 312.

3. Christian D. Larson. <u>Your Forces and How to Use Them</u>. London, E.C. 4: L.N. Fowler & Co. Ltd., (1961) 22.

4. <u>A Course In Miracles</u>. (Tiburon, CA: Foundation for Inner Peace, 1985) 198.

5. <u>Ibid, 198.</u>

6. <u>Ibid, 472.</u>

7. <u>Ibid, 291.</u>

8. NIV Bible, John 14:12.

9. Ibid, 1 Corinthian 12:12-27.

Other Books By the Author

- There's Nothing Going On But Your Thoughts -
  Book 2

- There's Nothing Going On But Your Thoughts -
  Workbook

- Class/retreat information at www.helengordon.com.